Words of Wisdom

Inspirational Quotes and Thoughts
on Optimism, Success, Fear,
Overcoming Failure, Persistence, and
Resilience that Will Change Your Life

Marc Reklau

Disclaimer

This book is designed to provide information and motivation to our readers. It is sold with the understanding that the publisher is not engaged to render any type of psychological, legal, or any other kind of professional advice. The instructions and advice in this book are not intended as a substitute for counseling. The content of each chapter is the sole expression and opinion of its author. No warranties or guarantees are expressed or implied by the author's and publisher's choice to include any of the content in this volume. Neither the publisher nor the individual author shall be liable for any physical, psychological, emotional, financial, or commercial damages, including, but not limited to, special, incidental, consequential or other damages. Our views and rights are the same:

You must test everything for yourself according to your own situation talents and aspirations

You are responsible for your own decisions, choices, actions, and results.

Marc Reklau

Visit my website at www.marcreklau.com

"The path to success is to take massive, determined actions." —Tony Robbins

Marc Reklau

Introduction

I have wanted to write this book for a long time. I have loved inspirational quotes since I was very young. I wrote them all over my school books and notebooks at a young age. They reminded me of the good things life had waiting for me.

Inspirational quotes gave me hope and comfort in the tough times when I was facing loss, failure, or rejection. The words of wisdom of the greatest people gave me the power to go on.

I have never read the whole works of the great philosophers; not even Shakespeare: Just the ones they forced me to read in high school. My fascination with these great thinkers came when I read their quotes, which proved to be eternal wisdom. I like and admire Ralph Waldo Emerson, Thomas Alva Edison, Albert Einstein, Benjamin Franklin, Henry Ford, Walt Disney and all the others based solely on their quotes. That might be a mistake. It doesn't matter. Their words and phrases kept me going when things looked dire. That's why in my first book, 30 DAYS, every chapter opens with one or two quotes.

Inspirational quotes always gave me that shot of energy, hope or motivation just when I needed it.

When I became jobless at the end of September 2013, I was full of fear. I didn't know what I had coming, so the first thing I did was google "Fear quotes." I printed them out and had them next to me all the time.

At the same time, I was building my business, which was supposed to be a coaching and consulting business but became something entirely different over the years.

My Japanese translator told me I should put in some work and publish a book with the motivational and inspirational quotes that had helped me most on my way, from being jobless to international bestselling author, and here we are.

May these quotes give you the energy, motivation, inspiration, hope, and comfort they gave to me.

Just remember one thing: If you are looking for real change, reading the inspirational quotes is not enough. You have to get to work after reading them.

That will make all the difference.

I will leave you with some the greatest thinkers of all time (and Winnie the Pooh). May they inspire you and bring good things to your life.

1

Every adversity, every failure, every heartache carries with it the seed of an equal or greater benefit.

Napoleon Hill

Once you can embrace this truth, everything changes. The fear of failure disappears because from failure, something even greater grows, such as a bigger win or a greater love. There is nothing more to fear. You can try it right now. Look back at your heartaches, your losses, your failures. Did something better come of them? I bet that if you really look for it, you will find it.

2

The only thing worse than being blind is having sight but no vision.
Helen Keller

What a powerful truth—even more so coming from a blind woman. Everything starts with a vision. If you don't have a vision, you just get by. You float around, living a life mostly dictated by others—by your boss, your parents, your spouse, your circumstances. Once you have a vision for *your* life and *your* goals, everything changes.

What's your vision? Where do you see yourself in five years? Create that vision. Hold it high in your thoughts and then find the tools you need to start your journey to make your vision a reality.

3

Forgiveness is the art of admitting that I am like other people.
Mother Theresa

Forgiveness is one of the most powerful forces of the universe. We follow all the advice and exercises of self-help or personal development books, but when we are stuck, it often comes down to a lack of forgiveness. The lack of forgiveness is one of the biggest energy and success blockers out there. Once we let go of our grudges and start forgiving others—and ourselves—incredible changes begin to happen.

4

The fool doth think he is wise, but the wise man knows himself to be a fool.
Shakespeare

Some wisdom is simply eternal. If you look around, you'll see that it's still true. If we think we already know everything, we start losing. I know it. I've been there. However, if we adopt the mindset of the eternal apprentice, know that there is always more to learn, and are keen on learning more, then not only are we wise, but we also show one of the two characteristics extraordinarily successful people show: They always want to learn more and keep asking questions.

5

Keep away from people who try to belittle your ambitions. Small people always do that, but the really great make you feel that you, too, can become great.

Mark Twain

Have you noticed that Mark Twain's words are still valid? I've been blessed to meet many more great people and successful people in the last few years. They never belittle you but encourage you to follow your path. It's the mediocre people who belittle you or don't answer your emails—maybe because they fear that you'll be better than them one day. Use Mark Twain's word as comfort when somebody belittles you or ignores you and then become so good that they can't ignore you anymore.

6

The harder you work, the luckier you get.
Thomas Jefferson

This is one of my favorite quotes. For many years, I thought other people were just more talented or luckier than me. But once I started taking my life in my own hands and working on a better future, I noticed the same thing: The more I worked, the luckier I got. When people ask me if luck was part of my success, I struggle to come up with an answer. To call it luck would undermine the hard work I did. Maybe there was a bit of magic to it, too, but 98 percent was hard work, overcoming rejection, learning from failure, and persistence, persistence, persistence.

7

There are no great people in this world. Only great challenges which ordinary people rise to meet.
Admiral William Halsey

Too many times, we feel ordinary. Small. Without power. We think that leaders are born. That genius is genetic. And that we need a special talent to do great things. So we sit on the sidelines and watch how the big game called life is played. If we are "lucky," we notice one day what admiral Halsey knew many years ago: that all great things are done by ordinary people like you and me who rise to the occasion. If you're thinking, "Oh, that's not me," remember that doing great things is often doing small things in a great way. When will you start?

8

Whatever you can do or dream, you can begin it. Boldness has genius, power, and magic in it.
Goethe

I know. It sounds too good to be true, but one of the secrets to success and happiness in life is to start. Start following your dreams. Just talking about it is not enough. Magic happens when you follow your dreams. Things will suddenly begin to fall into place. You will start to naturally attract the right people, the right opportunities, and the right resources, and incredible things will start to happen. Nothing attracts success more than somebody who is doing what they love.

9

If you want to know what a man is like, take a good look at how he treats his inferiors, not his equals.

J.K. Rowling

The real character of a man (and a woman) is shown in the way he treats others. Said more straightforwardly, the person who treats you well and treats the waiter bad is not a good person. Think twice if you want to go into business with a person like this.

Do you have people like this in your surroundings? Watch them closely. The most charismatic people treat all people the same and show them the respect they deserve. Sometimes, they treat the people they can expect the least from the best. That's true greatness. Treating the janitor with the same respect as the CEO is what great leaders are made of. Remember this.

10

When you have exhausted all possibilities, remember this. You haven't.
Thomas Edison

Blessed be Thomas Edison. If you want to overcome failure and fear of failure once and for all, listen to him. His quotes helped me over and over again when I was ready to give up—and there were many times. He also shows us the secret to success, which is also one of my favorite quotes: "Our greatest weakness lies in giving up. The most certain way to succeed is always to try just one more time."

11

The greater danger for most of us is not that our aim is too high and we miss it, but that it is too low and we reach it.

Michelangelo

The danger is that if you set your goals too small, you'll end up in mediocrity. But if you aim very high and miss, you still might have taken your life to the next level. I always advise setting huge goals. Even if you miss, you'll be better off than before. The only condition is that you celebrate your progress and don't torture yourself for not reaching the goal. One thing that doesn't show in Michelangelo's equation is that if you continuously set small goals and achieve them, you might still succeed in the end and not be trapped in mediocrity. It's up to you.

12

Imagination is everything, it is the preview of life's coming attractions.
Albert Einstein

Everything starts "in your head"—in your imagination. Next year's vacation, the new car, the new computer: it's created in your imagination before you take action in real life to get it. And so are your goals and your ideal life.

Imagination is a very powerful weapon of mass creation. If you imagine a positive environment or use your imagination to go back to the most wonderful moments in your life, you can create this happiness in the present. If you use your imagination to see your coming vacation, to see yourself there, you create happiness in the moment. If you want to reach a certain goal, use your imagination to visualize it and take inspired action to materialize this goal.

Warning: simply imagining and daydreaming about your goals is not enough. You have to go get them.

13

It took me twenty years to become an overnight success.
Eddie Cantor

We often look at "overnight successes" and want to be like them. We want to be the basketball player, the Olympic medal winner, the bestselling author, the actor, and we think all we need is luck. We just need to sit in a café, and Hollywood will discover us. Or if we could just play on the team, we'd score the same goals. What we don't see is the enormous sacrifice behind all these "overnight successes." Twenty-three-time gold medalist Michael Phelps practiced six hours a day, seven times a week for many years. Michael Jordan got up at six in the morning and practiced his shooting after not making his high school team. John Grisham wrote an hour every day before starting his day job as a lawyer over the years. It might not take twenty years to become an overnight success, but let it be at least two, three, or five..

14

The difference between the impossible and the possible lies in a man's determination.
Tommy Lasorda

You can say it louder but not clearer: the difference between winning and losing, between the impossible and the possible, lies in determination. It's a question of attitude. When the going gets tough, your determination will make the difference. Will you give up in the face of adversity, or will you keep going? Will you give up when life deals you some bad cards, or will you play these cards the best way possible? Will you listen when people tell you, "That's not possible. You can't do it," or will you tell them, "Step aside and watch me while I'm doing it"? Everything was once impossible. It was determination paired with vision, desire, and execution that made it possible. Your turn. Make your choice.

15

There are no shortcuts to any place worth going.

Beverly Sills

One of today's biggest misunderstandings is that people want a quick fix. "Three steps to happiness!" "Three keys to financial freedom!" The problem is there is no quick fix, and thinking that there is leads to more unhappiness. No wonder we have higher depression and suicide rates than ever before.

Happiness is possible for you. Financial independence is possible for you. But you have to be ready to do the work, be patient, and fail over and over again. You will have to take rejection over and over again, but in the end, you will succeed. If you waste your time looking for the shortcut, you will be doomed. Yes, you *might* win the lottery. But did you know that statistically, you have a better chance of being struck by lightning? I'm just saying.

Stop searching for the shortcut and start working on your goals now. Your future self will thank you.

16

The sweetest pleasure arises from difficulties overcome. Publius Syrus

We all want a life free of problems and difficulties where everything goes our way, and we get everything we want. Unfortunately, few of us have a life like that—except on social media. But stop a minute and think back. Wasn't it the difficult times that shaped you most? Didn't you learn life's most important lessons from the difficulties you had to overcome? Didn't your confidence grow every time you managed to overcome obstacles and solve problems? Aren't difficulties and overcoming them exciting? Weren't your biggest losses the seeds for your greatest victories? Remember, it's the biggest storms that make the best sailors, not the calm waters.

17

I think whether you are having setbacks or not, the role of a leader is to display a winning attitude.

Colin Powell

Science has proven that our attitudes are more important for winning than talent, genius, or anything else. Setbacks are a normal part of life. They will come sooner or later. As the leader of your life, you must maintain a winning attitude, knowing that you will prevail in the end. You have overcome setbacks before, and you will do it again. Having a winning attitude means that even when you face a loss, you are convinced that you'll win in the end. Sometimes, learning from a short-term loss can set you up for an even bigger long-term victory

18

Gratitude will shift you to a higher frequency, and you will attract much better things.
Rhonda Byrne

Gratitude is, without a doubt, one of the most powerful forces of the universe. And yes, if you count your blessings, you will see (or attract) more things to be grateful for because what you concentrate on, you'll see more of. The benefits of writing down three things you are grateful for are countless. It's even scientifically proven that an "attitude of gratitude" leads to increased optimism, increased happiness, better sleep, and better relationships. Grateful people are also less prone to depression or anxiety. If gratitude came in pill form, we'd all run to get it. Yet we can have all these benefits simply sitting down for a couple of minutes every day and counting our blessings

19

A superior man is modest in his speech, but exceeds in his actions.
Confucius

Actions speak louder than words. There are too many people just talking and not enough people doing. If you want to impress people, stop talking so much about what you are going to do and start doing it. Let your actions and results do the talking. Don't brag about how generous you are but donate to charity. Don't talk about what a great spouse, daughter, or son you are but be one. Don't tell your boss what a great worker you are but let your work and your numbers speak for themselves. (Some bosses can't see your great job, so you may have to brag about it, but that's the exception, not the rule). Be modest in your speech and generous with your actions.

20

People are always blaming their circumstances for what they are. I don't believe in circumstances. The people who get on in the world are the people who get up and look for the circumstances they want, and if they can't find them, make them.

George Bernard Shaw.

Circumstances are overrated. We often use "our circumstances" as an excuse for not getting something —or even worse, not even trying. It is scientifically proven that our outside circumstances make up only 10 percent of our lives and happiness. Where we live, where we are from, and who we are with only have a small influence on what we make of our lives. So, you have two choices: you can complain about your circumstances and not do anything, or you go out and make your own circumstances. If you look at successful people, that's what they did, and you can do it too. Look to the people who are where you want to go, look at how they made their circumstances, and then do the same.

21

Remember no one can make you feel inferior without your consent.
Eleanor Roosevelt

It often seems like "the others" are to blame if something happens to us or we feel offended. *They* offended us. *They* made a remark. *They* were ridiculing us. But when we shift from the external to the internal, everything changes. What "they" say to us is one thing. How we respond to it is another. Being called an idiot can only offend you when you think deep inside that you are an idiot. If you know you're not, you might as well laugh it off. If you feel inferior to somebody else, it's because you allowed it. The good news is you have the power not to feel inferior. It's up to you. The basis is healthy self-esteem. Know that you're not inferior to anybody on this planet but also not superior. You are you. Remember this the next time somebody "makes" you feel inferior.

22

In a world that is changing quickly, the only strategy guaranteed to fail is not taking risks.
Marc Zuckerberg

Not taking risks was a strategy that is always guaranteed to fail, but even more so nowadays. In a time when you could stay at a job for twenty-five years, not taking risks might have been a guarantee of survival and getting your pension in the Western world, but those days are over. Nowadays, not taking risks means staying stuck, not progressing, being left behind. If you want to reach new horizons, then you have to take some risks. There are many roads to success, but there is only one road to failure: not doing anything and not taking risks.

23

Face the worst. Believe the best. Do the most. Leave the rest.
Bishop Mel Wheatley

This quote is a surefire strategy for living a good life in fifteen words. Face the worst. It's an inevitable part that bad things happen to good people, so be prepared by knowing that overcoming our worst experiences often contains the seed of our most significant growth. Believe the best. Believe that you'll make it. You can do it! Good things are waiting for you. Do the most. Do the best you can with what you have at any given moment. That's it. That's enough. Not more, not less. Leave the rest. If you adhere to the first three phrases of the saying, the fourth will fall into place. Things will happen, and you can't change them. You only can accept them. Leave the rest. You'll be fine.

24

It is one of the blessings of old friends that you can afford to be stupid with them.
Ralph Waldo Emerson

Our personal relationships are the number one predictor our of future happiness. Science has found out that healthy personal relationships not only make us happier but also help us live longer. A vital ingredient is our friends. It's a blessing to fall back on a support network with whom we can simply be ourselves, make stupid jokes if we like, and laugh until tears roll down our cheeks. They say a true friend knows all your weaknesses and still likes you. We often don't have more than four to five real friends—that is, those who are always there, those who you can call at three in the morning and find an open ear. Choose your friends wisely.

25

The hardest arithmetic to master is that which enables us to count our blessings.

Eric Hoffer

It might be hard, but once we dominate the arithmetic to count our blessings, our whole lives will change. The power of gratitude is one of the most powerful forces in the universe, and once we start counting our blessings, we start becoming aware of how many we have in our lives. There are so many things we take for granted. We don't cherish them until they are gone. Are you grateful for your health? For being able to get up every morning? For being given a chance to live another day on this beautiful planet? For your spouse? For your children? For your friends? Start counting your blessings every morning, and your life will never be the same.

26

Great minds have purposes, others have wishes.
Washington Irving

Which group do you belong to? Do you just wish for a better life? Are you daydreaming about what your life could be like? Or do you have a purpose? A big why? Something that makes you jump out of bed every morning instead of hitting the snooze button on your alarm clock. If you already have a purpose, you know what to do. You know where you're going, and having a purpose will help you achieve your goals, even if everything seems to go against you. If you're still searching for your mission, stop every now and then and listen to your heart. Ask yourself, "What is my purpose?" and don't be afraid of your answer. You probably already know what your purpose is. All you have to do is stop wishing and start following it.

27

We suffer more often in imagination than in reality.

Seneca

How many of your worries have become a reality? Let me guess. Less than 10 percent? Most of the time, we suffer because of something we did or said in the past that we can't change or because of something that could happen in the future but probably won't happen. We are suffering most of the time while losing the most important moment: the present. There is no suffering in the present.—no worries, no fear. To become more aware of the fact that pain is mostly happening in your imagination, write down all your worries and problems. Then erase all the problems that are in the past and that you can't change anymore, all the problems that are in the future and haven't happened yet, and all the worries that you have no power over, such as the economy and politics. Now, look at what's left on your list. I'd dare to say that there's probably not much.

28

It is during the darkest moments that we must focus to see the light.
Aristoteles Onassis

You'll see more of what you concentrate on. That's why once you listen to a song, it seems to be played on all the radio stations, or when you want to buy a new red car of a certain type, you suddenly see that car everywhere. Use it to your advantage. You control your life experience by controlling your focus by controlling where you put your attention. If you want to see more light, focus on the light. If you want to see more happiness, focus on everything you can be happy about right now. If you have fallen, focus on your future goal, and get up and go for it. In the darkest moments, focus on how you have overcome problems and have been strengthened by them. Focus on growth.

29

Optimism is the one quality more associated with success and happiness than any other.
Brian Tracy

More than a decade of research in the fields of positive psychology and neuroscience confirms what Brian Tracy told us years ago: we become more successful when we are happier and optimistic. Optimistic salespeople, for example, sell a whopping 56 percent more than their pessimistic counterparts. Other studies show that optimism can make CEOs 15 percent more productive. They also have healthier teams that perform better. But it doesn't stop there. Happy and optimistic managers can improve customer satisfaction by 42 percent. So yes, learning to interpret events optimistically leads to much higher success and more happiness, and it strengthens our biological and psychological immune systems. Optimists even live longer. The best thing is that optimism can be learned.

30

To accomplish great things we must not only act but also dream, not only plan but also believe.

Anatole France

If you want to accomplish great things, then acting is not enough. You must also dream. The dream will keep you going when things become difficult. But dreaming is not enough because dreaming alone doesn't get things done. You must also act. The best plan is not good enough if you don't believe you can achieve it. And believing by itself will not get you there if you don't know where you are going. Dream, act, plan, and believe. Every single action by itself is not enough. If one of the ingredients is missing, then it will be difficult to achieve your goals. It's the sum of the four that will get you anywhere.

31

Failure is simply the opportunity to begin again, this time more intelligently.

Henry Ford

If you want to get ahead of life, then failure is inevitable. The greatest success stories are often the stories of people who have overcome significant failures. It's not a failure if you keep trying. That's how Oprah ended up having her own TV channel after being fired from a news station at the beginning of her career for "not being suitable for TV." That's how Michael Jordan went from not playing on his high school basketball team to becoming the greatest player of all time. Failure is not the end. It's just one way that you learned how not to succeed. There are countless stories of successful people who turned their failures into successes by starting again more intelligently.

32

The optimist sees the rose and not its thorns; the pessimist stares at the thorns, oblivious of the rose.
Kahlil Gibran

What you concentrate on. You'll see more of. The rose and the thorns coexist. So do triumph and drama, success and failure. Will you go through life as an optimist, always concentrating on the positive things around you, and thus, create paradise on Earth? Or will you interpret your world as a pessimist, only concentrating on all the bad stuff around you and creating your own hell on Earth? The only difference between optimists and pessimists is the way they interpret situations and events. Which way will you choose? Choose wisely.

33

First say to yourself what you would be; and then do what you have to do.
Epictetus

The contents of countless self-help books are reduced here to one sentence. Epictetus provides us with a simple instruction manual for a good, successful, and happy life. First, say to yourself what you could be. Who do you want to be? What do you want in life? For most of us, we don't even have an answer to these questions. And if we have, we forget the second, more important part: do what you have to do. Once you know who you want to be, trace a plan and plot out the actions and steps you have to take to become this person. Yes, it really is that easy. Get clear on who you want to be, make a plan, get to work, and become that person.

34

It's never too late to be that you might have been.
George Elliot

What are your dreams? When did you give up on them? We live in the best time ever to make your dreams come true. The opportunities are countless. Who do you want to be? What do you want to do? Get clear. Make a plan and start working on getting there. You can make your dreams come true. Start today. Drop the excuses, such as "I'm too old," "I'm too young," or "I live in the wrong country" and get to work. You can search for inspiration on the internet. Surely, there already are people living your dream. Let them inspire you. If they can do it, you can do it too. Go. Become the person you want to be.

35

Man cannot discover new oceans unless he has the courage to lose sight of the shore.

Andre Gide

If you want to venture into new experiences, if you want to change, if you want to improve your life, if you're going to leave your "comfort zone," then chances are that you have to take some risks. You have to have the courage to step into new, uncharted territory in your life. It's scary, but it will be worth it. As they say, "The magic happens outside of your comfort zone." It's true. Once you dare to step out of your comfort zone, exciting things happen—growth happens. Give it a try. You won't regret it.

36

Challenges are what make life interesting: Overcoming them is what makes life meaningful.
Joshua Marine

What would our lives be without challenges? Boring. It's the contrast that makes life interesting. Sun and rain. Cold and warm. Success and failure. Challenges and overcoming them. Think back to your biggest challenges. Weren't those also the events that defined you as a person and that made you grow? Who would you be without these challenges? Would you have come as far? Would you be who you are today? I doubt it. Embrace the challenges life throws at you and make the best out of them. That's what life is all about.

37

Be not angry that you cannot make others as you wish them to be, since you cannot make yourself as you wish to be.

Thomas Kempis

Did you ever try to change other people? You can stop right now. It's impossible. You cannot change people by telling them what to do. But you can change yourself. You can be the change you want to see in the world. You can be an example and inspire people to change because they want to follow you. Don't tell people to go to the gym. Go to the gym yourself. Don't force people to read more. Read more yourself. Don't tell your kids to eat healthier. Eat healthier yourself. When we leave our egos at the doorstep, everything gets so much easier.

38

Spend more time smiling than frowning and more time praising than criticizing.
Richard Branson

What a straightforward nugget of wisdom that will automatically improve your relationships, your happiness, and your life. If you smile, many people will feel attracted to you, love to have conversations with you, and just love to be around you. The same goes for praise. Every person on this earth is hungry for recognition and appreciation. People leave their jobs, wives leave their husbands, and husbands leave their wives due to a lack of acknowledgment. If you had two friends—one that frowns and criticizes, and one who smiles and praises—who would you spend your time with?

39

Self-conceit may lead to self-destruction.

Aesop

Self-conceit is so dangerous. It makes us lose our grit, our enthusiasm, our work ethic. It makes us relax because we think we are already there. It makes us deliver 10 percent less than possible, not giving our best. Self-conceit not only may but most definitely will lead to self-destruction. The most dangerous time when self-conceit might crawl in is just when you are having success. Suddenly, you might think, "That's it. I've made it. I'm on top." The problem is that right when that you feel like you've made it and that there's nothing more to do, you start losing. Stay hungry, keep pushing, and don't lower your guard.

40

Don't judge each day by the harvest you reap but by the seeds that you plant.
Robert Louis Stevenson

This change in perspective can turn a really bad day into a really good day. How? Well, sometimes we get into situations where things just don't happen. We worked a lot, and the results are just not showing. It's easy to fall into the trap of thinking "nothing is working" or "this will never work" if we judge our days by the "harvest we reap"—a.k.a., the results. Take the same day and judge it by the seeds you planted. Did you make contacts, send offers, or meet new people? Yes? Well, then it was a good day, and sooner or later, the seeds you planted will bloom and bring you the results you need. Don't judge your days only by the results you get. Judge them by all the plants you seeded for your future success. This idea puts everything in perspective.

41

Enthusiasm spells the difference between mediocrity and accomplishment.
Norman Vincent Peale

Sometimes, when everything seems to be going against us, the only thing that keeps us going is enthusiasm. The word enthusiasm stems from the Greek word *enthousiasmos*, which means "possessed by a god, inspired." It would be easy to give up and return to the anonymity and comfort of mediocrity. Why complicate our lives through struggle, pain, and sacrifice? Those who are enthusiastic know the answer: because it will be worth it. The accomplishment that comes after the suffering will be worth the sacrifice. To get us through such times, the only thing we have is our enthusiasm. We go after our goals, and we don't even know why, but something keeps us going. Maybe because we are "possessed by a god" and inspired not to give up. Enthusiasm keeps us going.

42

If we had no faults of our own, we should not take so much pleasure in noticing those in others.
La Rochefoucauld

Why is it so easy to see flaws in others and not in ourselves? Why do we always know what others should do with their lives but have no idea what to do with our own? From the outside, it's always easy to know what's right or see other people's faults. Seeing other peoples' faults seems to comfort us in our own inadequacy. Maybe we should just stop judging others and work on our own mistakes. Surely, there's a lot of work to do for each one of us to do, and we wouldn't have so much time to interfere in other people's lives and point out their mistakes if we focused on ourselves instead.

43

The deepest craving of human nature is the need to be appreciated.
William James

Appreciation is so important. We are humans. We want to be admired. We want to be acknowledged. We want to be appreciated. When we are appreciated, we function better under any circumstances. Even science has proven that we learn more and become better and more productive when we are praised and acknowledged. People simply respond better when they are appreciated. Conversely, a lack of appreciation damages relationships with our bosses, our marriages, and our friendships. It's so easy to appreciate people. As a result, they will respond better and cooperate a lot more willingly with us. Acknowledgment, praise, and gratitude never fail and change our relationships and our lives for the better.

44

The meeting of preparation with opportunity generates the offspring called luck.

Anthony Robbins

What seems like pure luck to the observer is often the result of many hours, months, or even years of preparation. When the opportunity arises and you are prepared to take it, it looks like you've been lucky. But you've actually worked hard toward this moment for a long time.

There will always be someone who will call it luck. It's easier and a great excuse for them to not get to work on their own goals. If it's all down to luck, then they don't even have to try. Those who know will know it was preparation that made the seizing of the opportunity possible in the first place.

45

The only good luck many great men ever had was being born with the ability and determination to overcome bad luck.

Channing Pollock

Determination is the greatest type of "luck" to have. If you have the ability and determination to overcome "bad luck," then nothing can stop you. Life is a rollercoaster with its highs and lows. Some things will work out fine, and others won't. The most important thing is to keep your determination—to overcome the bad moments. In the end, luck is only a matter of perspective and focus. If you think you're lucky, then there's a higher chance you will be. If you think you have bad luck, then you'll see proof of it everywhere. That's how focus works. If you think you're lucky, you're right, and if you think you're unlucky, you're right. Choose your thoughts wisely.

46

We delight in the beauty of the butterfly, but rarely admits the changes it has gone through to achieve that beauty.

Maya Angelou

Change is messy and scary. Most of the time, we only see the end result—the success of a person, the finished product—and then we want the same and forget that it has probably been a long, hard road, a process. It's like a larva turning into a cocoon and turning into a butterfly. We look at the butterfly and say, "How beautiful," but we forget the long change process the larva had to go through to become that butterfly. If we only had the same patience with our own change progress. We could become what we always wanted to be. Next time you are close to giving up, remember the larva on its way to becoming a butterfly. In the end, all the sacrifices will be worthwhile.

47

Life is thickly sown with thorns, and I know no other remedy than to pass quickly through them. The longer we dwell on our misfortunes, the greater is their power to harm us.

Voltaire

Life is full of setbacks, problems, and challenges. They are inevitable. They are part of life. Period. You have two choices: pass quickly through them, accept them as part of life, and solve them or dwell on them, pity yourself, stay stuck in the problem (as if that would solve it), and not let go. If you choose the second option, if you ruminate and dwell on your misfortunes, they will harm you and might spin you into a downward cycle. This is dangerous territory for your mental and physical health. Learn to let go. There is absolutely no sense in dwelling on the past. It will only hurt you. Pass quickly through.

48

The greatest pleasure in life is doing what people say you cannot do.
Walter Bagehot

There is really nothing better than doing the things people said you cannot do, is there? If you know that you can do something and people tell you otherwise, use the fact that they do not believe in you as additional fuel. Tell them to step aside and watch you do it. The best thing is if you did it once, you can do it again and do more and more things that people once thought you couldn't do. All great stories start with one person doing something that other people said they couldn't do. What do people say you can't do? Why not go out and just do it?

49

Every time you are tempted to react in the same old way, ask if you want to be a prisoner of the past or a pioneer of the future.

Deepak Chopra

If you keep doing what you are doing, you'll keep getting what you are getting. If you want to change things in your behavior, you have to start doing new things. You have to become aware of your old behavior and what triggers it. If you react in the same old way over and over again, you will become a prisoner of your past and won't be able to change your behavior. If you *decide* (yes, everything starts with a decision) to react differently—in a new way—you become the pioneer of your future and initiate real change. It's not easy, and you might have to practice a while, but it will be worth it.

50

Life is too short to be little. Man is never so manly as when he feels deeply, acts boldly and expresses himself with frankness and fervor.
Benjamin Franklin

Don't let others belittle you, and above all, don't belittle yourself. Life is too short for that. Give yourself permission to be human, feel deeply, and be true to your emotions. Be brave and act boldly according to your values. Don't be afraid to be you. Be authentic. Say what you mean and mean what you say. Develop a passion and live the life you always wanted to live. Time flies. Start now.

51

Mickey Mouse popped out of my mind onto a drawing pad 20 years ago on a train ride from Manhattan to Hollywood at a time when business fortunes of my brother Roy and myself were at lowest ebb and disaster seemed right around the corner.

Walt Disney

Don't give up. Sometimes, something can develop in your direst moments when everything is going against you and "disaster seems right around the corner." It's often right in these moments that we can develop our greatest potential. It's like something is pushing or helping us.

Don't misunderstand me. Don't just sit there and do nothing, waiting for a miracle. What seems luck or a miracle is often the result of relentless and tireless work over the years. So keep working and don't give up. Your miracle might be just around the corner.

52

Anyone who stops learning is old, whether at twenty or eighty. Anyone who keeps learning stays young. The greatest thing in life is to keep your mind young.
Henry Ford

Shawn Achor mentions in his book "The Happiness Advantage" that when scientists were studying extraordinarily successful people—in this case, graduates of Harvard Business School—they found that the most successful 10 percent had two characteristics in common that distinguished them from the others. First, they believed in themselves. They believed that they would make it happen. They believed they could be successful. Second, they never stopped learning. They were always asking questions. They always wanted to know more. Adapt this success mentality of the eternal student, always wanting to learn more. It will make you successful and keep your mind young.

53

Love is the master key that opens the gates of happiness, of hatred, of jealousy and most easily of all, the gate of fear.
Oliver Wendell Holmes

All we need is love. Love is one of the most powerful forces in the universe and can heal everything. But it works both ways. It also makes you vulnerable, and great love for someone or something can often turn into great hate. Why do divorce settlements come to mind now? Where there is love, there is jealousy. However, we need to ask if there is jealousy in *true* love, or if jealousy is connected to low self-esteem.

Last but not least, love opens the gate of fear—fear of losing the beloved person, fear of betrayal, fear of sickness.

What can we do? Add more love to the formula. While love is the master key to all these painful emotions, it's also the best antidote for them. Be careful. We're talking about *real*, unconditional love, not the romanticized and idealized love of Disney and Hollywood movies, which doesn't exist in reality.

54

Somewhere along the line, we stopped believing we could do anything. And if we don't have our dreams, we have nothing.
Charles Farmer

When and where did you stop believing in yourself? Can you pinpoint the moment? Remember that belief in themselves is one of the two characteristics of extraordinarily successful people. Without an unshakeable belief in yourself, everything is more complicated, and achieving your dreams becomes nearly impossible. Without your dreams, you have nothing, as Charles Farmer says.

Dreams give us hope, but just dreaming is not enough. Start believing in yourself again, have dreams, and then take actions that consistently bring you closer to your dream until your dreamed life becomes your real life. It all starts with believing in yourself. Start today.

55

Small deeds done are better than great deeds planned.
Peter Marshall

Some people spend their days just talking about everything they are going to do "one day." They make great promises and grand plans but never act. They only talk, talk, talk. Their real contribution to the world is *nothing*. And then there are other people who don't speak so much. They just keep doing small things. A smile, a kind word, a tiny contribution to charity. These are the people who are actually changing the world through their actions. No big talk, just small deeds. They what they can with what they have. Nothing more, nothing less.

Who is making a more significant impact? Of course, it's the second group. Actions speak louder than words, or as Ralph Waldo Emerson once said, "Your actions speak so loud I can't hear you." Don't be a talker. Be an action-taker. The world will thank you for it.

56

When you are offended at any man's fault, turn to yourself and study your own failings. Then you will forget your anger.

Epictetus

Funnily, it's always easier to see other people's faults and not notice our own. Epictetus gives us a genius recipe. From now on, whenever you are offended by another person's fault, look to yourself. Why is it bothering you so much? Other people are such a great mirror for us. What we don't like about them is mostly something we don't like about ourselves—something we have too much of or something we lack. Self-reflection always returns us to inner peace and happiness. We must "study our own failings" or ask ourselves, "Why does this bother me so much?" Every time something in others annoys us, we'll find out the reason, get to know ourselves better, and yes, totally forget what angered us in the first place.

57

Good luck happens to people who work hard for it. Sometimes people just fall into the honey pot, but I've consistently strived to create whatever good fortune I can get in my life and consistently strive just as hard not to screw it up once I have it.

Patrick Duffy

Scientifically, there is no luck. Richard Wiseman studied "lucky" and "unlucky" people and came to the following conclusion: "In science, there is no such thing as luck. The only difference is whether or not people think they are lucky or not. Whether they expect good things or bad things to happen to them." Seemingly your attitude and expectations have more to do with your luck than anything else. Sometimes, people just seem to be lucky, but if you take a closer look, you'll see a hard-working person who takes chances, fails, and tries over and over again. The end result seems like luck when it's only the logical consequence of doing the right thing over a long period of time. It's the outcome of a process or a journey.

58

Good luck is when opportunity meets preparation, while bad luck is when lack of preparation meets reality.
Eliyahu Goldratt

Many people consider luck to be opportunity meeting preparation. The message is to be prepared. Prepare yourself as much as possible so that you are ready to take the opportunity when it comes. Lucky people are also able to transform their bad luck into good fortune always by seeing the positive side of their bad luck. They are convinced that any bad luck they're having will work out for the best in the long run. They don't dwell on their bad luck but search for ways to be prepared to prevent more bad luck in the future. Capitalizing on opportunities is purely a matter of focus! When we are stuck in negativity, our brains are literally incapable of seeing opportunities. If we are positive, then our brains stay open to seeing these opportunities when they appear and seizing them.

59

I've found that luck is quite predictable. If you want more luck, take more chances, Be more active. Show up more often.

Brian Tracy

Richard Wiseman and many other positive psychology researchers have found that a huge difference between lucky and unlucky people is their attitude and willingness to take chances. While people who consider themselves as unlucky shy away from taking any risks and putting themselves out there, people who consider themselves lucky are always out there, taking small, calculated risks and taking chances. Lucky people create, notice, and act upon the chance opportunities in their lives. They build strong networks and have a relaxed attitude towards life while being open to new experiences. Unlucky people think they are powerless and depend on destiny or God's will. Once again, it is more about the approach we take than about coincidence. Try the first approach.

60

I believe life is a series of near misses. A lot of what we ascribe to luck is not luck at all. It's seizing the day and accepting responsibility for your future. It's seeing what other people don't see and pursuing the vision.

Howard Schultz

I mentioned earlier that what we consider as luck hugely depends on other factors, such as our attitudes, our expectations, and if we feel lucky. Studies show that "lucky people" do see things that people who consider themselves as unlucky don't see. In one study, researchers asked subjects to count photos in a newspaper. Those who considered themselves lucky took mere seconds to solve the task, while the unlucky ones took an average of two minutes because they didn't see a very large message on the second page that said, "Stop counting. There are forty-three photos in this newspaper." They also failed to see another message that said, "Stop counting and tell the experimenter you have seen this, and you win two hundred and fifty dollars." People who claimed to be unlucky in life looked right past this opportunity. Stuck in the negative focus, they were incapable of seeing what was clear to others.

61

Every really new idea looks crazy at first.
Alfred North Whitehead

Mahatma Gandhi said it many years ago: "First they ignore you, then they laugh at you, then they fight you, then you win." With a new idea, it's kind of the same. First, they think you are crazy; then they ridicule you—they might even try to undermine you. Then the idea becomes the new normal. They say they should have come up with it, and then they copy you. If people are telling you that you are crazy, you might be on the right path. Many times, being creative and coming up with new revolutionary ideas means going against the grain. The more revolutionary, the crazier you might seem. It happens to the best of us. Don't let the naysayers win.

62

The trouble with most of us is that we'd rather be ruined by praise than saved by criticism.
Norman Vincent Peale

We all like praise, and most of us don't like criticism. It's totally normal. Praise makes us feel good, happy, accepted, and acknowledged. Criticism hurts and makes us feel inadequate, not worthy, and small. Of course, It's always better to praise people than to criticize them, especially when we want to build lasting relationships, but Norman Vincent Peale is right. We can be ruined by praise. If people only praise us all the time and don't mention our shortcomings, then we might lose our way and be on the road to perdition. But if our surroundings are full of critics, the same might happen. We might not even dare to try things just because we don't want to be criticized. The truth—as always—is in the middle. The right dose matters. Surround yourself with people who don't criticize you but have one or two people of confidence around you who tell you "the ugly truth" every now and then and save you from being ruined by praise.

63

Love yourself first and everything else falls into line. You really have to love yourself to get anything done in this world.

Lucille Ball

Love yourself like your neighbor. We often see the good in others and fail to see it in ourselves. The most important relationship that you have in this life is the one you have with yourself. If you don't like yourself, how can you expect others to like you? How can you expect to love others if you don't love yourself first? Many problems we have stem directly or indirectly from self-confidence—the salary raise we don't get, the appreciation we don't get, the relationship we don't find. Once you learn to love yourself, everything else falls into place. How do we do it? By accepting ourselves as we are, recognizing our intrinsic value as people, knowing that we deserve respect, and overcoming perfectionism. That's it. Not more, not less.

64

Let us always meet each other with smile, for the smile is the beginning of love.

Mother Theresa

People subconsciously decide if they like us or not in a couple of seconds. Do you know how you can make most people be friendly, cooperative, and polite in those first few seconds? Smile! Give every person you meet your most sincere smile. A smile can do miracles. Have you ever tried it? Smiling is contagious. In most cases, people will smile back and be kind to you. It really is the beginning of love. Nobody can resist sincere politeness, a good heart, and a smile. Smiling is also good for your health. Last but not least, smiling sends a signal to your brain that things are all right. One study has even found a link between smiling and longevity. Smile and smile a lot.

65

A person's faults are largely what make him or her likeable.
Anne Lamott

Accepting your flaws is one part of being authentic, being you. Have you ever noticed that the most successful people are the ones who are authentic? They are not playing any roles. They are who they are. They know their strengths and weaknesses and accept their faults. They have no problem being vulnerable and taking responsibility for their mistakes, nor do they fear the judgment of others. It's funny—the less you try to please others, the more they will like you. The more you are yourself, the more people will be attracted to you. Permit yourself to be your authentic self. The rewards will be awesome.

66

Only put off until tomorrow what you are willing to die having left undone.
Pablo Picasso

That unwritten e-mail, the old friend you want to reconnect with, that time you want to spend with your family, that trip you want to take: don't put it off anymore. One day, it might be too late. Many of us live our lives eternally leaving things for later. "I'll do it when the kids are out of the house," "when the next project is done," "when I get the promotion," "when I retire," and so on. And then comes the day when we don't have time to do it anymore. Start living *now*. Do the things you always wanted to do *now*. Make plans *now*. You are not guaranteed another decade, another year, or even another day. Only put off the things you are willing to leave undone when you die.

67

Have no fear of perfection, you'll never reach it.

Salvador Dali

Perfectionism is the source of frustration, inferiority complexes, anxiety, and in the worst case, depression. It's one of the top things that prevent people from living a happy and fulfilled life. What a waste of energy. Stop trying to be perfect. You never will be. The best thing is you don't need to be perfect to be great. Just do the best you can with what you have at any given time. That doesn't mean you shouldn't analyze the mistakes you make or your failures, but you can skip the beating yourself up part.

How can you overcome perfectionism? Easy. One, accept yourself as you are. Two, learn to love yourself and forgive yourself. Three, take extremely good care of yourself.

Get rid of perfectionism from today on. Don't take my word for it. Take one of the greatest artists in history's word for it.

68

You don't have to see the whole staircase, just take the first step.
Martin Luther King

We get lost many times on our way. We often don't know what the future will bring. In these times, it will be useful to remember Dr. King's wisdom. When you are totally overwhelmed, blocked, and frozen and don't know what to do next, follow this recipe for moving on: only think about the next small step you can take. What's the next small thing you can do or have to do? Do it. After that, do the next small thing you can do right now. And then the next one. You don't need to see the end result. You just need to take the next step. Step by step, you'll move forward. One step at a time, you will work your way to success. Take that first step.

69

Everything you've ever wanted is on the other side of fear.
George Addair

Whenever you feel fear, think of this quote. Become aware of your fear. When does it come up? What does it want to teach you? What is in it for you if you overcome your fear? What's on the other side of fear? Analyze the facts. Ask yourself, "What's the worst thing that can happen to me if I do this?" Then evaluate if the risk is worth taking or not. It's highly probable that the greatest opportunities wait for you beyond your fears. Don't let fear be the red light that makes you stop. Let it be a yellow light that warns you. Once you know yourself better and have overcome your fear over and over again, you might even turn it into a green light. Every time fear comes up, you can think, "I must be onto something great if fear kicks in. Green light. Go, go, go!"

70

Fear is not real. It is a product of thoughts you create. Now do not misunderstand me, danger is very real, but fear is a choice.
Cypher Raige

Face your fears! Ninety percent of them are pure imagination, a product of your thoughts. They're illusions! Incredible stories of drama and disaster that will probably never happen made up by your mind —"the world's greatest director of soap operas," as T. Harv Eker says. They're a survival mechanism your mind uses to try to keep you safe and in your comfort zone. The problem is that great things such as development, growth, and success happen outside of the comfort zone.

Don't take your fears too seriously. Anything that your mind doesn't know about scares it, and that's when fear kicks in. Danger is real. Fear is not. Ninety percent of the time, there will be no real danger when fear comes up. If that's the case, go for it!

71

Aim for the moon. If you miss, you may hit a star.
Clement Stone

Set ambitious goals. As Michelangelo says, "The greater danger for most of us lies not in setting our aim too high and falling short, but in setting our aim too low, and achieving our mark." Think big. It's scientifically proven that people who set goals are generally more successful. Having goals makes us achieve things we didn't even dare to dream of. Focusing on a goal brings forth internal and external resources that are necessary for getting there, and then things begin to happen inside us, as well as around us. There's only one thing: self-punishment is not allowed. If you don't reach your most ambitious goal, you may still "hit a star." Regroup, analyze, and go again. Celebrate how far you have come instead of beating yourself up for a near (or not so near) miss.

72

Learn from the past, set vivid, detailed goals for the future, and live in the only moment of time over which you have any control: now.
Denis Waitley

Everything happens in the present moment. If you live in the past, you'll stay stuck and might become frustrated or even depressed. If you live in the future, you will miss all the great opportunities that are happening right now. Learn from past experiences, forgive yourself, forgive others, let go, and move on. Set vivid, detailed goals for the future: They will motivate you and give you the drive you need to succeed. Live in the only moment that is important—the present moment. The only moment in which you can work on your goals is always now. What you are doing right now will become and define your future.

73

The bitterest tears shed over graves are for words left unsaid and deeds left undone.
Harriet Beecher Stowe

Live your life like today was your last day—of course, *with responsibility*. Don't go out and party hard and get drunk, but if you want to do something, *do it*. Don't postpone it to next week, next month, or next year. If you want to say something nice, *say it*. Don't wait for a "better occasion."

Taking that leap is the best way to live. There's nothing worse than not telling a person how you feel about them, and then they're gone, and you can't tell them anymore because "the next time I see them" doesn't come. Do it *now*. Don't postpone all the good deeds you want to do. The best time to do it is always *now*. Live like that. Live a life with no regrets. As a wise man once told me, "Never regret the things you did, only those you never tried."

74

God gave man two ears and one mouth, so listen more and talk less.
Jewish Proverb

How much better would the world be if we would just follow this proverb? Listen more, talk less. The harsh reality is that most people never listen. Better said, they listen to answer and not to understand what's being said. As soon as the other person starts talking, they are already thinking about how they are going to respond. That's not listening, my friend. Good listeners always have the advantage over good talkers because they always allow people to hear their favorite speaker in the world: themselves. Learn the art of listening profoundly. The more you listen, the smarter you will get. People will also like you better. Why? Because you'll be of a rare breed. Next time you are having a conversation, listen to the person in front of you while giving them your full attention.

75

A hero is no braver than an ordinary man, but he is braver five minutes longer.

Ralph Waldo Emerson

We often think that you have to become a superhuman to do extraordinary things or be an extraordinary person to become a hero. But when we watch closely, we see that extraordinary people are ordinary people doing extraordinary things, that heroes are no braver than ordinary people but just braver for a little bit longer. You can become extraordinary, too, by doing extraordinary things, going the extra mile, and being extraordinarily kind. Being extraordinary is not about genetics. It's about your habits, your values, your beliefs, your daily routines, the people that are around you, and the environments you are in. If one person has done it, another person can do it too.

76

The biggest mistake people make in life is not trying to make a living at doing what they enjoy most.
Malcolm Forbes

The latest studies confirm what Malcolm Forbes said decades ago. Around 70 percent of the current workforce is unhappy with their jobs. "Making a living at doing what you enjoy most" is easier said than done. It takes a lot of courage to decide to leave the rat race behind and do what you enjoy most. It might not be easy, but it's definitely worth it. Think about it. You spend more time at your job than with your loved ones. That has an enormous impact on your life. Thanks to the internet, there are more opportunities than ever. You don't need to quit your job cold turkey. You can start something on the side—a business, teaching something, or writing a book—and work on it from eight to eleven every night instead of watching nonsense on television. Maybe one day, your side hustle will allow you to quit your job.

77

If you have made mistakes, even serious ones, there is always another chance for you. What we call failure is not the falling down, but the staying down.

Mary Pickford

The biggest mistake is the fear of making one. Many people stay stuck because they are afraid of making a mistake. They are so afraid of mistakes that they'd rather do nothing. Everybody makes mistakes. The question is not how to avoid mistakes but how to deal with your mistakes. Do you keep making the same mistakes, or are you learning from them? What exactly are you learning from them? Accept your mistakes as feedback and keep going. If you want to reach new territories, you have to take the risk of making some mistakes along the way. Mistakes don't matter as long as you're not making the same mistakes over and over again. Don't be afraid of mistakes. Don't be scared of failure. It's only failure if you stay down.

78

Many of life's failures are people who did not realize how close they were to success when they gave up.
Thomas Edison

It's a tragedy. Many people just give up a little bit too early. If they would have pushed a little more, if they would have hung in there just a little longer, they would have succeeded. Thomas Edison is an expert in failure. He didn't consider his ten thousand attempts at making the light bulb failures. He said, "I just found ten thousand ways how not to make a light bulb." When you're close to giving up, think of Thomas Edison's recipe for success: "Our greatest weakness lies in giving up. The most certain way to succeed is always to try just one more time." Think of the gold digger who stopped digging just twenty centimeters before hitting a rich vein of gold. Don't give up. If things get tough, it's almost definitely a sign that you are close to success. Push a little harder and see what happens.

79

It is hard to fail, but it is worse never to have tried to succeed.
Theodore Roosevelt

It's better to try and fail than to never try. What are you afraid of? Why won't you at least try? If it doesn't work out, nothing changes. Okay, it might hurt a little, but you'll get over it and do better next time. It's a hundred times better to ask the girl for a dance, to apply for the job, to go to the tryout than live the rest of your life with the thought, "What would have happened if … ?" Yes, failing is hard, but the pain goes away. Learn from your mistakes and go again. The pain of failure will never go away entirely, but it will hurt less every time. The fear of failure is worse than failure itself. If you really want to succeed, you have to fail every now and then. This change of attitude will change everything.

80

Experience is the word people use to call their mistakes.
Jewish Proverb

The question is not if you'll make some mistakes in your life. The question is how you deal with them. Are you repeating the same mistakes over and over again, or are you learning from them? If it's the latter, congratulations! You're moving forward. You're gaining valuable experience. You're getting better. Just do the best you can at any given time. Not more, not less. Analyze your mistakes. If you can correct them, do so; if not, accept them, let go, and promise yourself that you won't repeat them. It's only a problem if you keep repeating the same mistakes over and over again. Remember, success is the result of the right decisions, the right decisions are the result of experience, and experience is the result of the wrong decisions.

81

It is far better to be alone than to be in bad company.
George Washington

Walk away from relationships that don't nurture you anymore. Walk away from people who don't value you. Walk away from negative people. Life is too short to spend it in bad relationships with people who suck the happiness out of you. Yes, it often takes more courage to walk away than to stay in a bad relationship, but you can do it. Don't let loneliness drive you into a relationship. There is nothing worse than being lonely in a relationship. Be with people who support you and value you. Less is often more. Also, in the relationship and friendship department, choose quality over quantity. Have a few high-quality relationships instead of many superficial ones.

82

A bad partner is worse than rain – the latter makes you go home, while the former makes you go outside.
Jewish Proverb

Choosing the right partner is crucial for all your future endeavors, and a lot of your future success will depend on it. The person you are around the most has a huge influence on you. Choosing a happy partner is extremely important because the person you are with affects your happiness and success tremendously. Studies show that our relationships are the number one predictor of long-term happiness. The one thing that all extremely happy people have in common is good interpersonal relationships. Unfortunately, it also works the other way around. Being around negative people can seriously damage your self-esteem and self-confidence. Choose your most important relationship wisely.

83

We don't develop courage by being happy every day. We develop it by surviving difficult times and challenging adversity.

Barbara De Angelis

There will be challenges, adversity, and difficult times in your life. There's no way around it. And we are afraid of them because tough times really put us to the edge. We all prefer the better times when everything is smooth and easy, but it's the tough times that shape us. The more obstacles we overcome and the more difficult times we survive, the more times we look our challenges right in the eye and say, "Bring it on," and the more confident we become. That's when courage is born. It's the knowledge that we can deal with things, the knowledge that we can deal with the next curveball life throws at us and countless others that might come and that we will become stronger and stronger and more and more courageous.

84

Fortune always favors the brave and never helps a man who does not help himself.
P. T. Barnum

Fortune always favors the brave. Look around you. There are so many cases that it must be true. It seems like the braver they are, the luckier they get. We often have to take a risk to move forward. If we don't take risks, we stay stuck in our comfort zones. You know, where it's nice and cozy and, well, comfortable. But nothing ever happens. Progress doesn't happen in the comfort zone. Growth, improvement, and development demand we take risks every now and then. When we take (calculated) risks, fortune favors us. If you want to make sure that you succeed in life, don't count on anybody's help. Help yourself first, and then help might come from other places—God, the universe, fortune—but you must first help yourself.

85

I really believe in the old expression that what doesn't kill you makes you stronger. It's through adversity that you find the strength you never knew you had.

Christie Brinkley

Nietzsche said it, Kelly Clarkson sings it, and science has proven it: "What doesn't kill us makes us stronger." This is a fact. It's a truth. But it only works if you choose the path of growth, gratitude, love, and forgiveness. What do you think about Christie Brinkley's quote? Is it true for you? Is it true for most people you know? It's in the face of adversity where character is built. Bad things happen to good people. It's the ability to learn from the bad things in life that will define you and make you become an even better person. It's all good, even the bad things, if you make it so. I'm 100 percent convinced that you can.

86

Adversity has the effect of eliciting talents, which in prosperous circumstances would have lain dormant.
Horace

Don't get me wrong. I prefer positive experiences by a thousand times, but when the going gets tough, you can only become strong and get through it when you know that you will learn from it and might even be grateful that it happened because something good came out of it. It's amazing how we show our biggest potential in the toughest situations. We suddenly show characteristics we didn't even know we had. As strange as it sounds, adversity often brings out the best in us. The way someone deals with the circumstances life throws at them makes all the difference. The way you deal with adversity makes all the difference. Make the best of it. You can do it. People are doing it right now at this very moment. If they can do it, you can do it.

87

A lot of people think I hard such a rosy career, but I wanted to identify that one of the things that helps you have a long career is learning how to deal with adversity, how to get past it. Once I learned how to get through that, other things didn't seem so hard.

Cal Ripken

When you look at the most successful people, their lives were often not a walk in the park. Many times, their life stories are full of struggle, hurt, and even abuse. Somehow, they rose above it and kept going. You can do the same by seeing your situation as something that makes you grow, not as something that will break you. That is not easy to do, and you will need a lot of guts to make it through, but you can. They made it through, so you can make it through. If you develop resilience—the art of getting back up on your feet over and over again after being knocked down—you'll have it all. Nothing and nobody will be able to stop you. You know how resilience is built? Practice! Falling down over and over again and getting up over and over again. Getting better at it and getting stronger every single time.

88

The greatest battles you will ever fight are with yourself, and you must always be your toughest opponent.
Jewish Proverb

Your biggest enemy and your biggest critic is not somebody from the outside. It's the person you see every morning in the mirror. Nobody will criticize you more harshly, and nobody will be harder on you than that person. The secret to a happy and successful life is to find the balance between "being your toughest opponent" with a healthy measure of self-criticism and not falling into the exaggerated and destructive self-criticism most of us have at one point in our lives. This battle is a lifelong one, but you are in it to win it. Self-criticism is good because it keeps you from falling into self-complacency, but don't exaggerate it because that would be as self-destructive. Find the balance. As always, "the dose makes the poison."

89

A successful man is one who can lay a foundation with the bricks others have thrown at him.

David Brinckley

The way to success is often a journey you have to walk alone. You'll often have to go against the grain and against what society, your friends, and your family tell you. Somehow, they already seem to know the right path for you. On your way to success, you'll meet with failure and rejection many times. It's how you meet those obstacles that will make all the difference. Will the bricks life and others throw at you knock you down, or will you use them to lay a firm foundation? If it's the latter, a successful life is guaranteed.

90

Two men looked out from prison bars, one saw the mud, the other saw stars.
Dale Carnegie

Your perspective defines everything. You can create your own heaven or hell on this earth, depending on what you choose to concentrate on. Do you see the mud— the negative, the pain, the crises, everything that's not working well—or do you see the stars, always focusing on the good in every situation, the learning experience, the positivity that is all around you? Here lies one of the secrets to leading a happy and successful life: your perspective. What are you choosing to concentrate on? Experiences t are neutral until we start to give them meaning. Your vision of the world and your perspective decide if something is good or bad. What may be a great tragedy to some could be a wakeup call for others to take their lives into their hands and thrive.

91

Twenty years from now you will be more disappointed by the things you didn't do than by the things you did.
Mark Twain

Don't let your fears limit or paralyze you. Try things even if you fear failure. You only live once. At the end of your life or even just twenty years from now, there's a high probability that you won't regret the things you did, only those you never tried. When Bronnie Ware, an Australian nurse who accompanied the dying on their last days on our beautiful planet, interviewed the dying, they told her that they didn't regret the things they did. Rather, they regretted the things they didn't do and didn't allow themselves to do— like being more authentic, living their own lives and not the lives other people wanted for them, staying in touch with friends, living a happier life, spending more time with family.

Live your life now, and try the things you want to try. That's what you will remember twenty years from now. No regrets.

92

Optimism is the faith that leads to achievement. Nothing can be done without hope and confidence.
Helen Keller

Optimism is the key to success. It's scientifically proven that optimism enhances your performance and achievement. Optimistic salespeople outsell their neutral or pessimistic counterparts by 56 percent. Optimism improves your productivity, and optimistic managers can even raise customer satisfaction a whopping 46 percent. Optimists even live longer. And the best part is that optimism can be learned because, in the end, the only difference between optimists and pessimists is how they interpret events. Hope and confidence are crucial in any endeavor. Without them, we are lost. Cultivate optimism. It's worth it.

93

Life is 10% what happens to you and 90% how you react to it.
Charles Swindoll

A common misconception is that our external circumstances make up our entire lives and that we are slaves to them. In reality, they dictate only 10 percent of our future happiness and success. Yes, you read that right. Your external circumstances make up only 10 percent of your life. The other 90 percent is decided by you. What do you make of these circumstances? How do you react to them? What will you do when shit happens? Complain about the smell or use it as fertilizer? It's up to you. That is one of the greatest powers that we have. Jewish psychologist Victor Frankl considered it "The ultimate human freedom … to choose one's attitude in any given set of circumstances." You may not be able to control the circumstances that life presents to you, but you can always choose your response to these circumstances, and by doing so, have a massive impact on your life.

94

Life is a lottery that we've already won. But most people have not cashed in their tickets.
Louise Hay

You already are a winner. You are on this planet because you won a race against 250 million competitors. That's the lottery you've already won. Now make the best of it. Tragically, most people take something as beautiful as life for granted. They're stuck in jobs they don't like and in relationships where love left a long time ago. They spend time with people who don't support them. Wake up! Cash in your lottery ticket and live! This is not a dress rehearsal. You only have *one* life. One at bat. Do the things you always wanted to do. It might be difficult at first, and you might need a lot of courage, but it will be worth it. We've discussed it before. Never regret the things you've done, only those you never tried. Enjoy every day of this gift called life that was given to you.

95

The pessimist sees difficulty in every opportunity. The optimist sees opportunity in every difficulty.
Winston Churchill

It doesn't matter what happens to you in your life. What matters is the attitude you adopt. And the attitude you adopt is your choice!

They say that your life is the sum of your attitude and your decisions. Your attitude can dramatically change the way you see things and the way you face them. It can turn adverse situations in good ones and vice versa. That's why your attitude so crucial for your happiness.

Everything that happens to you is a challenge and an opportunity. It's up to you to choose how to take it. If you focus on difficulties, then you'll see them everywhere. If you concentrate on opportunities, then you'll see them when they come up.

96

Life is a grindstone. And whether it grinds you down or polishes you up is for you and you alone to decide.
Cavett Robert

Life is made up of laughter and tears, light and shadow. You'll suffer less if you just accept that as a fact. You'll be able to deal better with the bad moments if you change your way of looking at them. Even the worst situations have something positive, some learning experiences hidden within them. Search for it. Sometimes it takes some time to discover it.

Cavett Robert is right: there are situations in life that can make you or break you. The decision is yours. If you look at successful people, most of their lives were not a walk in the park. They overcame obstacles and tough situations. They decided to make the best of what was happening to them. If one person can do it, then so can you. William Shakespeare said it best: "There is nothing either good or bad, but thinking makes it so."

97

A man without a smiling face must not open a shop.
Chinese proverb

Smile! And smile a lot! A lousy attitude gets you nowhere. You may be able to hide it when working in an office or "behind the scenes," but in the front of the shop or the room, you can't. If you have a lousy attitude, your venture is doomed to go down in flames quickly. People don't want to buy from grumpy people. Smiling is contagious. Attitudes are contagious. So go out there and show the right attitude. When you are "on stage," put on your best smile. Don't tell me you can't do it. Ten thousands of Disney employees do it every day to create magic. If I haven't convinced you yet, just think of the other advantages that smiling has, such as improving your mental state and creativity. One study even found a link between smiling and longevity! Smiling people are perceived as more confident and more likely to be trusted. People just feel good around them. Smile and win in all relationships.

98

Every strike brings me closer to the next home run.
Babe Ruth

Fail over and over again. Babe Ruth's attitude is exemplary. If you can adopt his attitude, your success is secured. Many remember Babe Ruth as one of the greatest baseball players of all time and for his home run records. But few people know that the seasons when he had the most home runs were also the seasons when he had the most strikeouts. If you can internalize that way of interpreting failure, nothing can stop you. Twenty phone calls to make one sale? Good enough. Fifteen rejections for one big deal. I'd take it any time. Thirty job interviews to score your dream job? Bring on those interviews! Failure is how you learn, and overcoming failure is how you succeed. You know it's true because that's how you learned to walk, and that's how you learned to eat. Failing over and over again. Trying over and over again.

99

"I've missed more than 9,000 shots in my career, I've lost almost 300 games, 26 times, I've been trusted to take the game-winning shot and missed. I've failed over and over again in my life. And that's why I succeed."

Michael Jordan

When Dean Simonton studied the most successful scientists and artists through history, he found that they were also the ones who failed the most. Michael Jordan didn't become one of the best basketball players of all time because he played so well. That was only one part of the equation. The other part was that he was able to overcome failure like no other. The art is to take another game-winning shot after you just missed the last one, to overcome the fear of failure and try over and over again until you succeed. The art of always coming back, of always getting back on your feet, is what most matters. And this, my friend, you can practice. How? By failing over and over again.

100

People who pray for miracles usually don't get miracles. But people who pray for courage, for strength to bear the unbearable, for the grace to remember what they have left instead of what they have lost, very often find their prayers answered. Their prayers help them tap hidden reserves of faith and courage that were not available to them before.

Harold Kushner

Miracles do exist. The problem is that you can't count on them to happen when you need them. That's why it's far better to build the habit of resilience and bouncing back when you fall, the habit of courage to try over and over again, and the habit of persistence and not giving up, even if everything seems to go against you. Last but not least, one of the most impactful habits is the habit of gratitude, appreciating what you already have, and counting your blessings. Gratitude alone will make you more optimistic and more resilient. It's the antidote to all painful emotions. The more grateful, resilient, and courageous you become, the more probable are the miracles you search for. Just don't count on them.

101. I am thankful to all who said no to me. It is because of them that I'm doing it myself.

Albert Einstein

Sometimes, a "no" can be the best thing that happens to you. A no from a job opportunity can lead you to a better job. A no from a partner can lead you to a better partner. A no from someone else can lead you to do it yourself, as Einstein did.

We think we need somebody to start a business venture or a hobby with because we are insecure. Then we get a no, which is discouraging at first. But in the long run, maybe we notice that opening the business or starting the new hobby by ourselves is the best thing that could have happened to us. For J. K. Rowling, the rejection letters of countless editors and agents were a blessing because, after many rejections, she found a publisher that turned her *Harry Potter* series into a multi-billion dollar venture.

102

Life's six rules of success.
1.Trust yourself.
2.Break some rules.
3. Don't be afraid to fail.
4. Ignore the naysayers.
5. Work like hell.
6. Give something back.
                                    Arnold Schwarzenegger

If you look at successful people, you will find some characteristics over and over again in all of them. Who better to remind us than a man who was the son of a simple man in Austria and who went on to become the world's best bodybuilder, highest-paid movie star, governor of California. All of that with a name few can pronounce and an accent never heard before. He turned all his "weak points" into strengths and triumphed. Why? He had an unshakable belief in himself, he broke some rules, he failed over and over again until he succeeded, he surrounded himself with the right people and didn't listen to the naysayers, and (this is something we sometimes forget) he worked like hell. It's a recipe that you can also use. If you stick to it, it will work. When you have succeeded, it's time to give back.

103

Would you like me to give you a formula for success? It's quite simple, really: Double your rate of failure. You are thinking of failure as the enemy of success. But it isn't at all. You can be discouraged by failure, or you can learn from it, so go ahead and make mistakes. Make all you can. Because remember that's where you will find success.

Thomas Watson

If you want to be very successful, you'll have to fail a lot. Fail a lot, fail fast, learn fast, and go again. Yes, failure is not the enemy of success. We could even go so far as to say that there is no success without failure. Do like Thomas Edison did and fail yourself to success. Make mistakes and learn from them. The only thing you shouldn't do is make the same mistake over and over again. As long as you learn from your mistakes, you'll be fine.

104

Failure is a great teacher, and I think when you make mistakes, and you recover from them, and you treat them as valuable learning experiences, then you've got something to share.
Steve Harvey

So many dreams die because of the fear of failure. People are so afraid of failure and mistakes that they don't even try. True, failure is tough, and it hurts. But you know what's even worse? Never even having tried in the first place.

Nobody should arrive at his or her last hours wondering, "What if I had only tried this?" or "What if I had only tried to do that?" I'd rather try and fail a hundred times than carry these doubts with me to my death bed. What about you?

105

It's about how hard you can get hit and keep moving forward.
Sylvester Stallone

Let's get serious. Life will throw some serious curveballs at you. You might get knocked down every now and then. These parts of life are inevitable. Instead of being afraid of the tough times and going into hiding, accept the fact that you'll meet some challenges and take them head-on. You will get hit. What will make the difference is that you keep moving forward after getting hit and getting up after being knocked down? Every time you get knocked down and get up again, you will become better at it. You will become more confident, and in the end, you'll become unstoppable.

106

Perseverance is failing 10 times and succeeding the 20th.
Julie Andrews

If you ask most successful people for the one most important characteristic for success, they'll probably answer, "Perseverance." Perseverance is more important than talent, intelligence, and strategy. When we see the end result, we often think it's pure talent or genius. Then we look a bit closer and see that most success stories have one thing in common: perseverance.

When life doesn't go according to plan, keep moving forward, no matter how small your steps are. There is great virtue in never giving up. The top two habits that will determine success or failure, real change or staying in the same place are patience and perseverance.

107

You can never quit. Winners never quit, and quitters never win.
Vince Lombardi

It's highly possible that there may be some obstacles in your path before success comes. See the usual and inevitable setback as a temporary defeat and not as a permanent failure. Regroup, look for the learning experience, come up with a new plan, and try again. If the new plan doesn't work out either, change it and adapt it until it works.

Setbacks are when most people give up: They lack patience and persistence in working out new plans. Thinking of another inspirational quote may help you through the tough times. It has helped me a lot. Here it comes: "Our greatest weakness lies in giving up. The most certain way to succeed is always to try just one more time." Who said it? Thomas Alva Edison, of course.

Don't quit. Persistence is a state of mind. Cultivate it.

108

I'd rather attempt to do something great and fail than to attempt to do nothing and succeed.
Robert Schuller

Don't throw away your goal away at the first sign of misfortune or opposition. They are inevitable. Think of Thomas Edison and his ten thousand attempts to make the light bulb. Fail towards success like he did! If you fall down, get up, shake off the dust, and keep on moving towards your goal.

Mediocrity is easy. Playing small is easy. Hiding your talents is easy. Giving up is easy. Don't go the easy way. Dream big and fail big until you succeed big time. It will be worth it. Don't get to your last days with regrets, telling yourself, "If I only had tried."

I was very successful in not attempting anything. My life was also shit. Then I started to attempt great things. I failed a lot, and then I succeeded. It's a hundred times better to try and fail than to not try at all.

109

Plenty of people miss their share of happiness, not because they never found it, but because they didn't stop to enjoy it.

William Feather

In our search for happiness, we often forget that sometimes, we just have to stop to find it. It has been at our heels the whole time. Or maybe we are so obsessed with the big things that we forget to stop and enjoy the small things in life and the beauty all around us that bring us happiness. Enjoy the little things. Don't postpone life until you win the lottery, the kids are out of the house, the project is finished, or you get the promotion. Don't wait until retirement to do the things that make you happy. Stop for a moment, and enjoy happiness *now*. Smile, be grateful for what you have, go for long walks in nature, and meet up with your friends. What reasons do you have to be happy right now at this very moment?

110

Remember not only to say the right thing in the right place but far more difficult still, to leave unsaid the wrong thing at the tempting moment.
Benjamin Franklin

If you adhere to Franklin's wisdom, your relationships with other people will be excellent. Remember, you can say everything in the right tone and nothing in the wrong tone. The art is to find the right tone. Even more important is staying calm in the tempting moments. If it only were so easy. Countless relationships, marriages, and friendships have been ruined by not being able to leave the wrong thing unsaid at the tempting moment and simply keep the mouth shut. For the more emotional among us, it might take some practice, but it will be worth it. An old trick comes to mind: count to ten before you answer or leave the room. Don't send that email right away. Let it rest in your inbox for a day. It will be worth it.

111

You cannot change your destination overnight, but you can change your direction overnight.
Jim Rohn

Sustainable change takes time. It won't happen overnight. Make small changes every day that will lead to significant, lasting change over time. Small changes will bring you to your desired destination, to your desired goal. We have to stop thinking that we have to make massive changes to change our lives. This way of thinking leads us to be overwhelmed and paralyzed. Paralyzed by the magnitude of the task, we end up doing nothing and get stuck. But there is hope! We can start changing small things that don't require a huge effort right now, and those small changes will eventually lead to more significant changes and an entirely new destination.

112

Without hard work, nothing grows but weeds.

Gordon Hinckley

We live in such a fast-paced society where everybody wants to sell us the idea that success is easy and comes quickly and effortlessly. "Three steps to happiness!" "Become rich and wealthy in ten days!" So many people want to change their lives, but they don't want to do any hard work. They want the shortcut, the quick fix, and that's a recipe for disaster because the quick fix doesn't exist. There are no shortcuts to success, no magical systems. Change takes time. Becoming successful takes time.

The only secret to success is hard work. Don't let the get-rich-quick-schemes that are all over the place fool you. The only ones who get quick rich are the people selling these schemes to you. Without hard work, nothing grows but weeds.

113

Be the change that you wish to see in the world.
Mahatma Gandhi

This quote is maybe one of the most powerful ones in this book. Why? Because all the change in this world starts in one place: within you. You're not responsible for anybody else's behavior. You're only responsible for your own behavior. Set an example. Do you want to change the world? Start with yourself. Do you want your partner, colleagues, or spouse to treat you better? Treat them better. Do you want to be loved just as you are? Love others just the way they are. Do you want to save the planet? Start recycling, take public transport, and eat less meat. I'll repeat it: change starts with you. Try it.

114

Never give up, for that is just the place and time that the tide will turn.
Harriet Beecher Stowe

Many times, just before reaching a goal, things suddenly become difficult. It's like life, the universe, or God—whatever you prefer—wants to test us if we are really convinced, if we really believe, if we really have this deep-rooted faith that we can achieve our goal. Unfortunately, this is also the time when most people give up, like the often-mentioned gold-digger who is only inches away from the pot of gold and then stops digging. Keep this in mind the next time you are about to give up. You might be very close to achieving your goal. Just hang in there a little longer. Shift your perspective, and the next time things get difficult, believe that it might be the last resistance before your victory. By all means, don't give up!

115

When something is important enough, you do it even if the odds are not in your favor.
Elon Musk

When something is important to you, not doing is not an option. Giving up on the way is not an option. Quitting is not an option. If it's important enough to you, then you'll get energy from seemingly nowhere. There will be this voice inside you that will make you keep going. You'll fall down, but you'll get up again. You'll be on low energy, but you'll recover. You'll draw strength from somewhere. You won't listen to the naysayers and complainers. You will just go on in the direction of your goal.

The problem is that most people in our world never stop to ask themselves what's really important to them, and they just continue to do what they've always been doing—studying for a career they hate, staying in toxic relationships that have become stale.

Just between you and me, what is this incredibly important thing that you would do even if the odds were not in your favor?

116

The world is full of dreamers, there aren't enough who will move ahead and begin to take concrete steps to actualize their vision.
Clement Stone

Dreaming is important, but if you don't follow up with action, nothing will happen. If you put a deadline on a dream, it becomes a goal that you can reach. Instead of sitting around, waiting, and dreaming of a better life, take matters into your own hands and start taking action. The results will be nothing short of fabulous!

Your life is in your hands, so start acting on your ideas. By now, you have learned that doing small things consistently, you can get great results. Dare to follow your dreams, and you will find the power to achieve them. Start taking action now! The most significant difference between people who make their dreams come true and people who stay stuck is *action*. Stop dreaming. Start doing.

117

If you are going to achieve excellence in big things, you develop the habit in little matters.

Colin Powell

The way to great success, be it your job, your health, your finances, or any other endeavor, starts small. Do your best where you are and with what you have. Develop small good habits that will lead you to bigger good habits, and then you'll reach excellence. If you do the small things poorly, then chances are that you will do the big things poorly. If you're not happy with one thousand dollars, then you probably won't be happy with one million.

Excellence is a habit. Start developing it on the small matters.

118

The world is full of abundance and opportunity, but far too many people come to the fountain of life with a sieve instead of a tank car, a teaspoon instead of a steam shovel. They expect little, and as a result, they get little.
Ben Sweetland

Look for abundance and opportunity, and you'll see it everywhere. It's a matter of where you put your focus and what you decide to concentrate on. Don't buy into the scarcity mindset that the media and others want to sell you. There is enough for everybody if you only learn how to see it. Once you've found it, get out your tank and your steam shovel and serve yourself.
Life will give you what you expect from it, so always expect the best, and you'll often get it. Remember, you are in charge of your thoughts and beliefs. You can develop an abundance mindset. It might take a while, but it will totally be worth it.

119

Believe in yourself. Have faith in your abilities. Without a humble but reasonable confidence in your powers you cannot be successful or happy.
Norman Vincent Peale

Your beliefs will create your reality. Without a strong belief in yourself and your ability to achieve success, you'll find it very different to succeed. Beliefs are what distinguish the extraordinarily successful from the rest. The Pygmalion effect shows us that the more we believe in our ability to succeed, the more likely we are to do so. How do we believe in ourselves? It comes naturally to some people, while others have to work on it. Work on building this unshakable belief in yourself. It's the foundation of everything. Like everything else, it might take some time and some training, but you can work on it.

120

Do not wait; the time will never be just right. Start where you stand, and work with whatever tools you may have at your command, and better tools will be found as you go along.

George Herbert

I don't know who said it, but it hits the spot: "Waiting for the right moment to start something is like waiting to leave your driveway until all traffic lights are green." It will never happen. So many people lose opportunities or, even worse, their dreams because they are waiting for "a sign" or "the right moment," and they will never come. They spend their entire lives waiting while others start with what they have and improve along the way. The best moment to start something is always *now*. Take a leap of faith. It's better to start now and fail than wait your whole life for the right moment and end up asking yourself, "What if? What if I had only started this or that project? What would have happened?"

121

You can win in the late innings if you never quit.

Robert Forster

Don't give up. Period. You can win in the late innings if you are persistent and just keep going. J.K. Rowling was rejected a dozen times. She didn't give up. Today, she's a billionaire, and *Harry Potter* has his own theme park. That's only one of countless examples.

All you need is a clear goal and the burning desire to achieve it. Make a clear plan and act on it with daily steps, no matter how small they are. You have to be immune to all negative and discouraging influences. Last but not least, build a support system of one or more people who will encourage you to follow through with your actions and pursue your goals.

122

Perseverance is not a long race.; It is many short races one after the other.
Walter Elliot

Like so many times in life, what looks like one big thing is, in truth, a lot of small things lined up one after another. The same goes for perseverance. You don't have to compete in one long race. You'll be challenged over and over again, and you'll have to compete in one short race after another. You will fail every now and then and be really close to giving up. That's the point in the race when you have to ask yourself why you are in it in the first place. You might have to reset, readjust, refocus, and restart more than once. The most important thing is not to give up. That's perseverance.

123

Do something wonderful, people may imitate it.

Albert Schweitzer

Be an example. You cannot change others. The only thing you can to do is accept them as they are and be the best example and person you can be. Have you heard the idea that other people are like mirrors of us? The things we don't like about them are often things we have to work on ourselves or balance out. One of the most significant insights that my clients have is when they shift from "Others have to change," to "What if I change? Maybe then the others will also change." In most cases, that is precisely what happens.

Most of the people you meet will not listen to what you say, but they will imitate you and do what you do. Be the change you want to see in the world. Be an example.

124

Don't be pushed around by the fears in your mind. Be led by the dreams in your heart.
Roy Bennett

In your life, you will or won't do things out of either fear or love. Choose the latter. It will give you better results.

Fear is a very, very bad counselor. Unfortunately, we listen to it too much even though we should know by now that 90% of our fears are purely imaginary—self-produced stories of drama and tragedy that will never happen. When our dreams and beliefs are strong, there is no fear. When our dreams and goals lead us to take focused action, there is no fear. Listen to fear, but don't let it paralyze you. Don't let fear push you around! It might be your steady companion, so learn to do things in spite of fear. Susan Jeffers' slogan "Feel the fear and do it anyway" has helped me a lot.

125

We seem to gain wisdom more readily through our failures than through our successes. We always think of failure as the antithesis of success, but it isn't. Success often lies just on the other side of failure.

Leo Buscaglia

The fear of failure is the number one dream-killer in many people's lives, but why? Why are we so afraid of failure? Why can't we see it like Leo Buscaglia did? He tells us that success often lies just on the other side of failure. In other words, how would our lives change if we could see failure exactly like that?

Every failure, every heartache, every setback is necessary for growth and sets us up for success. Why not see it as a learning experience that makes us wiser and provides us with information and motivation? How would your life change if you could fully embrace the idea failure is a sign that points towards progress?

126

Discouragement and failure are two of the surest stepping stones in success.
Dale Carnegie

On your way to success, you will fail many times, and you will be tempted more than once to give up. It's normal, and it happens to most people. What makes the difference is what you do with failure and discouragement. Will you give up? Or will you accept them as part of the process, look for the learning experience, and use them as steppingstones? The choice is yours. Everybody falls down every now and then, but winners get up, shake the dust off, and keep going. They know that that's what it takes to succeed. If they can do it, you can do it.

127

The most important trip you take in life is meeting people halfway.
Henry Boye

Your success and happiness at home and in business depend on how you get along with other people. Success can mean something different to each person, but there is one common denominator: other people. The most successful people are often not the ones with superior intelligence or the best skills, nor are they more intelligent than others. They are the ones who have the greatest people skills.

Meeting people halfway is one of the most important skills, and it will go very far. People don't want to argue or our will or solutions forced on them. They want to be met halfway. It feels better.

128

Growth begins when we accept our own weakness.
Jean Vanier

Everybody makes mistakes. Everybody has flaws and weaknesses. The day you can accept them without justifying yourself or beating yourself up is the day that growth and improvement begins. To improve something, we must first acknowledge that it exists and that it can't be developed. It's tough to face the inconvenient truths about ourselves, but once we do so, we become invulnerable. It's funny, the more honest and vulnerable we become, the more invulnerable we become. When you accept your weaknesses, nobody can hurt you. The best way to silence your critics is to agree with them. Once you have accepted your flaws, you won't feel hurt anymore, and you can agree with your critics.

129

Be impeccable with your word. Speak with integrity. Say only what you mean. Avoid using the word to speak against yourself or to gossip about others. Use the power of your word in the direction of truth and love.

Don Miguel Ruiz

Don't underestimate the power of your words. The words that you use to describe your experience become your experience. Say what you mean and mean what you say. Speak the truth. Don't make false promises; they can kill your reputation. Words build relationships, but can also destroy them in no time.

Be careful with what you are saying not only about others but also about yourself. Maintain your inner dialogue positive. The way you communicate with yourself influences your whole life, your results, and the perception others have of you. Focus on what you want, not on what you don't want. Focus on truth and love. You will change your life by changing your language.

130

A little more persistence, a little more effort, and what seemed hopeless failure may turn to glorious success.
Elbert Hubbard

I might be repeating myself, but it can't be said often enough: don't ever, ever, ever give up. Things often get harder just before you achieve success. It's like the universe or God (whatever you believe) wants to test you. When you get to the point of wanting to give up, remember this quote. Just push a little more, just try one more time, put a little more effort into it. The difference between successful people and people who fail is that the successful ones tried a little harder and were a bit more patient and persistent. Try it, and you'll see.

131

Failure will never overtake me if my determination to succeed is strong enough.
Og Mandino

You can't fail if your determination to succeed and your belief are strong enough. Period. You'll find ways to overcome obstacles, and you'll see doors that open. This unshakeable belief in your success and your cause will give you the power to get up every time you fall—and you will fall. Just accept your mistakes and setbacks as feedback and learn from them.

Remember how you were when you were a kid. You learned to walk by falling down and getting up again. You learned to play sports by being bad at it and then improving over time. The time to change your mentality towards failure is now. Remember, it's only failure if you stop trying.

132

Never ruin an apology with an excuse.
Benjamin Franklin

Asking for forgiveness and acknowledging your mistakes shows greatness and strength, not weakness. Only the weak and mediocre can't ask for forgiveness. They think they have something to lose. They are also the ones who come up with excuses, and excuses ruin apologies. If you come up with excuses, the apology feels less real.

If necessary, genuinely ask for forgiveness. Swallow your pride and leave the excuses. You don't need to justify yourself. You're not weak. You're showing character. The right people will respect you more, not less, after you honestly apologize.

133

I can spot empty flattery and know exactly where I stand. In the end, it's really only my own approval or disapproval that means anything.
Agnetha Faltskog

You decide how people or what they tell you will affect you. They can only hurt or offend you if you allow it. Once you become aware of this truth and know exactly where you stand, a new life starts. You won't care what people think or say about you anymore. That's the beginning of a new freedom.

Most of the time, people are merely projecting their own problems on us, and it has nothing to do with us. If they tell you that you should exercise more, it's probably they who need to exercise more. If something affects you, look inside you and ask yourself, "Why does this affect me? Is there any chance I think this of myself too?" If there is, you can work on it. If not, it doesn't need to affect you. Easy, right?

134

Do the one thing you think you cannot do. Fail at it. Try again, Do better the second time. The only people who never tumble are those who never mount the high wire. This is your moment. Own it.

Oprah Winfrey

Doing something, failing at it, and trying (and failing) over and over again is the only way to learn and grow. That's just the way it is. The earlier you accept the fact, the better. Once you accept it, you can let go of the debilitating fear of failure that lives within each of us and accept that every failure is a great moment in our lives because they allow us to learn and grow. Isn't that liberating?

The only thing you have to watch out for is not persistently repeating the same mistake or persistently pursuing a plan that doesn't work. The difficulty might lie in distinguishing when to try again and when to change plans. Persistence means persistence toward achieving your goal, not persistence in doing the wrong thing over and over again.

135

I don't believe you have to be better than everybody else. I believe you have to be better than you ever thought you could be.

Ken Venturi

Life is not a competition. The only person you should compete with is the one you were yesterday, focusing on the person you want to become. It's not about beating others; it's about being content with yourself and improving yourself continuously. You don't have to be better than everybody else. Just do your best and enjoy the journey. Instead of competing with others, recognize your potential and strive for excellence. If you want to make life a competition, compete with yourself. Reach greater personal growth and achieve excellence in everything you want to do. You can do it.

136

When one door closes, another opens; but we look so often and so regretfully upon the closed door that we do not see the one which has opened for us.
Alexander Graham Bell

This quote is one that will help you most on your way to a successful and happy life if you can only believe it and build absolute faith in its truth. In your life, many doors will close. Friends will move away, you might lose a job or two, and lovers will leave you. But never forget that when one door closes, another opens—new friends, new jobs, new lovers. If you focus on the closed door, on the missed opportunities, you won't see the new great things that you can have in your life. If something ends, grieve if you must, but not for too long. Then, move on, look for what's coming, and above all, look for all the new doors (and windows) that are opening.

137

We make zero percent of the shots we didn't make.
Michael Jordan

You will never succeed if you don't even try. It's better to choose to try and miss than to not try at all. Yes, failing hurts. Trying and missing hurts. But missing opportunities because you haven't even tried hurt even more. We can always find excuses not to try. It's when we arrive at our last hours when the regret comes, and we ask ourselves, "What if I had taken the shot? What if I had tried? Would my life have been any different?" When you talk to people in their 80s or 90s, they usually regret the things they didn't do—the opportunities they didn't take. Learn from them.

138

Opportunity does not knock, it presents itself when you beat down the door.

Kyle Chandler

If you are waiting for an opportunity just to come around, you may wait for your whole life, and nothing will happen. You have to go out and look for opportunities and seize them at the right time. That might be scary at times, but remember, "Fortune rewards the bold and brave." Go out there and look for opportunities. Beat down a couple of doors and be prepared when you meet opportunity.

Many people do nothing and just wait for the opportunity to knock. They think that one extraordinary event will change their lives. They wait and wait, and nothing happens. But while they are waiting, they are missing all the small opportunities they could act on that could build up and accumulate into massive change, into the extraordinary thing they've been waiting for all this time. Don't sit and wait. Go out and beat down some doors.

139

Always believe that something wonderful is about to happen.
Coco Chanel

You won't always get what you want in life, but you surely will get what you expect! What a fantastic way to live life. The fun thing is if you live in the expectation of something wonderful happening every now and then, it will. That's the power of the Pygmalion effect, or the self-fulfilling prophecy. If you expect to be successful, chances are that you will be. If you expect a miracle around every corner, sooner or later, you will meet one. Beliefs are one of the strongest forces in the universe. They're one of the two characteristics that make the difference between the extraordinarily successful and the rest. They're the one thing you have to work on if you want a happy and successful life. Your beliefs create your reality. Believe.

140

Hard times don't create heroes. It is during the hard times when the hero within us is revealed.
Bob Riley

Don't misunderstand me. I love the good times—when everything goes smoothly and comes easily, and the sea is calm. But undoubtedly, it's the tough times that shape us and reveal our highest potential. That's when the hero we all have inside comes out. That's when we're suddenly able to do things we never thought we could do, deal with inhuman pressure that we never thought we were able to withstand, and overcome pain and sorrow we never thought was possible to overcome. Some invisible force seems to take over and make us stronger than we ever were before. When you go through hard times, remember these are the times that will provide the most significant growth and development. It can be tough, but you can do it alone or with help. You can do it.

141

The will to win, the desire to succeed, the urge to reach your full potential. These are the keys that will unlock the door to personal excellence.

Confucius

Do you want to know the rule for success? Confucius has given it to you: to be successful, you need the will to win, no matter how difficult the task and the road. This secret, together with an unshakable belief that you can succeed, will get you started.

You need a burning desire to succeed. This desire will help you overcome failures, rejections, and setbacks along the way—and you will have them. I'm sorry to say that there's no way around them. Setbacks are part of life.

Finally, you need the urge to reach your full potential, the urge to improve continuously, the urge always to learn more. This urge will make you strive for more instead of getting lazy and self-complacent when success shows up at your doorstep.

142

The key is to keep company only with people who uplift you, whose presence calls forth your best.

Epictetus

I heard this idea first from Zig Ziglar. He said you are the average of the five people you spend the most time with. If you examine your relationships closely, you might find that he's right.

Emotions are contagious. If you put three people in a room together, the most emotionally expressive one "infects" the other two with his or her emotions, no matter if the emotions are positive or negative. Your friends can be like springboards for your success, but they can also drag you down. Choose your company wisely. Stay around people who bring out the best in you and say "bye-bye" to the rest of them.

143

Beginning today, treat everyone you meet as if they were going to be dead by midnight. Extend to each person, no matter how trivial the contact, all the care, kindness, and understanding you can muster, and do it with no thought of any reward. Your life will never be the same again.

Og Mandino

If you choose this wise way of acting, life will never be the same, and the rewards will be beyond your imagination. It's a simple recipe that brings out the best in us. If you treat everybody you meet as if they were dead by midnight, there is only room for kindness, care, empathy, and goodness in all your interactions. There is no more room for animosity, envy, anger, or misunderstanding. What if you really lived that way? How would your life change? Why not try it? Why not now?

144

Iron rusts from disuse, water loses its purity from stagnation, even so, does inaction sap the vigor of the mind.
Leonard da Vinci

Everything changes with action. All the quotes you've read until now might motivate you. You might even say, "Oh, how wise _____ was." But without taking action, nothing will happen. The difference between successful and unsuccessful people or between dreamers and go-getters is *action*. Dreaming is not enough. Reading is not enough. But once you take action, everything changes. It goes without saying that, of course, you have to take action in the right direction. Also, don't mistake simple action with inspired action that follows a plan.

145

Do not wait to strike till the iron is hot; but make it hot by striking.
William Butler Yeats

There is a big myth out there—the myth that you have to be inspired or motivated to start doing something like writing a book or going for your goals. If you wait until you are motivated to start something, you might as well wait forever. Instead, start *right now* with what you have and go step by step towards your goal. Don't wait any longer to be motivated or inspired or for the time to be right. Start now! Make the iron hot by striking.

146

There is nothing else that so kills the ambitions of a man as criticisms from his superiors. I never criticize anyone. I believe in giving an incentive to work. So I am anxious to praise but loath to find fault. If I like anything, I am hearty in my approbation and lavish in my praise.

Charles Schwab

If more people had adopted Charles Schwab's philosophy, companies would run better, relationships would be better, and kids would grow up healthier. Why does it seem so difficult to praise but so easy to criticize? Criticism is simply useless because it has no benefits at all. It hurts people's feelings and their pride and even causes resentment. Praise, on the other hand, makes people who are doing their best more productive and simply better at everything they do because they want to achieve that high ideal we're holding for them. They want to become the person we already see them becoming. Between criticism and praise, always choose the latter. It will bring you many more benefits.

147

You can find a better you inside of you. Why don't you search for that?
Munia Khan

Let me tell you a big secret. You already have everything you are searching for. You already have the tools to get everything you want in life. I doubt that anything in this book is entirely new to you or that you have found a revolutionary new idea you had never heard before. Imparting brand-new information wasn't my intention. My goal was to remind you that you already have it all, and now comes the most challenging task: looking inside yourself and finding the tools and knowledge to change your life for the better and live the life you always wanted. It's all there.

It might be a bit uncomfortable to look inside yourself, and the programming you received from the first day of your life through your parents, teachers, religion, society, and television might turn down that inner voice that already knows everything. But listen to it. Listen a little closer. Can you hear it? It already has all the solutions.

148

Wealth consists not in having great possessions but in having few wants.
Epictetus

I don't know about you, but most people want to become rich or wealthy, right? For the longest time, we have thought that we need to accumulate possessions to become wealthy and happy. Maybe we should have read Epictetus' quote a long time ago. Perhaps it's not the accumulation of possessions but having fewer wants that make us really wealthy. It's already been proven that sometimes less is more; otherwise, why are there so many wealthy people with lots of possessions who are deeply unhappy? Above all, it depends on your definition of wealth, but if you have already tried the first option and it didn't work, why not try the second? It might work.

149

Dwell not on the past. Use it to illustrate a point, then leave it behind. Nothing really matters except what you do now in this instant of time. From this moment onwards, you can be an entirely different person, filled with love and understanding, ready with an outstretched hand, uplifted and positive in every thought and deed.

Eileen Caddy

Don't let your past define you. Your future is a clean sheet! You can start changing your life at any moment. Every day brings with it the opportunity to start a new life. You get to choose your identity at each and every moment. Right now, you can decide to become a different person and then put in the work and become this person over time. Yes, it's really that simple. You really are the writer, director, and main actor of your story. If you don't like how the story you call life is playing out, change it. Of course, it won't be super easy, and you might have to work hard, but you can do it.

150

Think big and don't listen to people who tell you it can't be done. Life's too short to think small.
Tim Ferriss

I'll let you in on another secret. Most of the people who did great things in their lives or even for our world were told, "It can't be done." Thank God they didn't listen to those people. Think big. The only limits are the ones you set yourself.

"Think big" doesn't mean you won't fail or that you won't have any setbacks along the way. It doesn't mean that you are guaranteed to reach your big goal. It doesn't mean that you won't meet frustration and rejection along the way. "Think big" simply means that you should chase your most significant goal. Go for it and have patience. Even if you come up short, you will undoubtedly be much further ahead than "thinking small" or "being realistic" would have ever gotten you (says the guy who went from jobless to an international bestselling author with more than twenty-five thousand readers in six years.)

151

I have yet to find a man, however exalted his station, who did not do better work and put for greater effort under a spirit of approval than under a spirit of criticism.
Charles Schwab

Charles Schwab knew it a hundred years ago, and science has been confirming it for years: praise and acknowledgment are basic needs. Millions of people are starving for praise and appreciation. When researchers asked people for their best day at work, the vast majority said it was a day that their bosses praised them. Other studies have proven that teams with managers who acknowledge and praise their work are up to 31 percent more productive. It's not rocket science. Just remember how you felt when somebody appreciated you. Didn't it brighten your day or even week? Don't spare praise and acknowledgment because they do miracles—and they're completely free.

152

A creative man is motivated by the desire to achieve, not by the desire to beat others.

Ayn Rand

Stop competing. Life is not a competition. The only person you should compete with is the person you were yesterday. Don't focus on others; focus on the person you want to become. Let becoming the best person you know you can be and the pursuit of excellence be your only motivation. Everything else is secondary. It's not about beating others; it's about achieving your dreams and your goals. It's about being content with yourself and improving yourself continuously. Stop competing. Stop feeling the need to become better than anybody else. Go for greater personal growth and spread happiness.

153

Either I will find a way, or I will make one.

Philip Sidney

If you embrace this attitude, nobody will ever be able to stop you. It's a surefire method to success. Either you find a way, or you make one. Remember that your success and happiness in life depend on your mindset and your beliefs to a huge extent. You can find a way and model yourself after people who have already achieved what you want, or you can create a new path. For example, g writers often say, "If the book you want to read is not written yet, maybe it's up to you to write it." If the path that you want to take isn't there yet, be the one who walks it for the first time.

154

If you set goals and go after them with all the determination you can muster, your gifts will take you to places that will amaze you.

Les Brown

One of the most powerful habits on your way to success is goal-setting. It will take you to places you never thought you could go. Most people overestimate what they can do in a month and underestimate what they can do in a year. Goals will drive you to take the right actions. They will lead you to your desired destination, like a GPS system. There's nothing like committing yourself to your goals, writing them down, and achieving them or even exceeding them.

Get clear about your goals, write them down, break them in small, realistic, achievable action steps, and go get them! See yourself reaching the goal over and over again (put a lot of positive emotion into that vision) and then get to work. The results will be amazing.

155

Fear and self-doubt have always been the greatest enemies of human Potential.

Brian Tracy

Fears and self-doubt are the number one dream killers. The way you deal with your fears and doubts will determine whether you become successful or stay stuck. Don't let your fears limit you or paralyze you. Fears are the mind's survival mechanism. Our minds want to keep us safe, and anything that they don't know scares them. Start challenging your fears. Ask yourself, "What's the worst thing that can happen to me if I do this?" Then evaluate if the risk is worth taking. You might find that the greatest opportunities will be behind those fears because most of the time, our fears are pure imagination. As Susan Jeffers says, "Feel the fear and do it anyway."

156

Most of the important things in the world have been accomplished by people who have kept on trying when there seemed to be no hope at all.
Dale Carnegie

Whenever you hit a roadblock or experience a setback, remember this quote. If you read a lot of success stories, you will see this pattern over and over again. Simply said, successful people are people who just stuck with their thing—their project—a little bit longer. In many cases, you will succeed if you just hang in a little bit longer. Remember Thomas Edison's secret to success: "The easiest way to succeed is always to try it just one more time." The art is to differentiate between when to let go and when to hang in there just a little bit longer.

157

What we achieve inwardly will change outer reality.
Plutarch

Your external circumstances are often a reflection of your inner thoughts and beliefs. If you want to change the outside, you need to change the inside—your inner beliefs and thoughts—first. It's a lot easier said than done, but it's the only way to bring on change.

Positive change will almost definitely not come from the outside, from others, or from life. If you want to become wealthier, healthier, and happier, you have to start from the inside. Believe that it's possible and then change your thoughts and beliefs. With the shift in your mindset and attitude, a change in your outer experiences and circumstances will follow.

158

Life is not always a matter of holding good cards, but sometimes, playing a poor hand well.
Jack London

Science has proven that your outer circumstances only define 10 percent of your happiness and well-being. Ninety percent is what you do with these circumstances. Life will not always go as planned, and it will probably throw you a couple of curveballs every now and then. That's just the way it is. No matter how many books you read or courses you take, you will never be able to control that. But you will always be able to control how you let those outer circumstances affect you and how you face them. Nobody can take this power from you. Just commit to the fact that no matter what cards life deals you, you will always play them the best possible way. That's all you need to do. Not more, not less.

159

There are no secrets to success. It is the result of preparation, hard work, and learning from failure.
Colin Powell

If you needed to hear it one more time, here you go: contrary to what people often want to sell you, such as how to "obtain big riches without working," "become a millionaire in thirty days," or "write a book and never work again," the ugly truth is that there is only one way to success. It's like Colin Powell says—success is the result of preparation, hard work, and learning from failure. Those are the basics. We could add patience, persistence, vision, belief, and goals, but if one of the first three ingredients is missing, your road to success will become more difficult or, in the worst case, be a road to failure. The good thing is you have the blueprint. Give yourself time, but start now. You can do it.

160

The best preparation for tomorrow is doing your best today.
Jackson Brown

We can talk a lot about future goals and learning from past experiences. We can complicate things, but we can also make them simple. If you do your best today, and if you do it every day, your future will be bright! There's no way around it. It's pure logic. You could probably have a great life even if you did your best only half of the time. We have to calculate the bad days and the sad days into the equation. And sometimes, your best will just be 50 percent or even 20 percent instead of 100 percent. This recipe will still work. Do your best today and every day, and your bright future will simply fall into its place. Don't you believe it? Why not just try?

161

Limitations live only in our minds. But if we use our imaginations, our possibilities become limitless.
James Paolinetti

The only limitations you have are the ones you on yourself. This concept is huge. It might take a while to grasp it, but once you embrace it fully, life will never be the same. If you look at the greatest artists, scientists, athletes, and businesspeople, you'll see people who have overcome those limits. Everything was once impossible until somebody made it possible. Roger Bannister was an English doctor and the first man to run the mile under four minutes. In a time when nobody had ever done it, and all the medical studies confirmed that it was not possible for humans, Roger Bannister knew that the limits were only in his mind. He built the belief that he could do it, and he kept practicing. Where are your limits? I dare you to challenge them.

162

Believe you can, and you're halfway there.
Theodore Roosevelt

If you want to achieve any endeavor, you must believe that you can make it. If you believe that you can do something, you're already halfway there. Then you just have to add work and persistence, and sooner or later, you will be there. If you don't believe, it will be a lot harder to achieve anything or do anything. If you don't believe in yourself, few other people will believe in you. Work on that belief.

In a study of extraordinarily successful people, the most successful people had two things in common that distinguished them from the rest: (1) they always wanted to learn more and were always asking questions, and (2) they believed in themselves. They always believed that they could do it. Become a believer in yourself.

163

If you don't like the road you're walking, start paving another one.
Dolly Parton

Sometimes things just don't work out. Other times, we are stuck in situations we don't like, but we keep doing what we have always been doing. Of course, if we keep doing what we were doing, we'll keep getting the same result: we stay stuck in the situations we don't like. If you are in a situation that you don't like, and it just won't change, start doing things differently. Pave another road. Change something—direction, behavior, habits, whatever. Pave another way. If not, you'll be stuck for another five years or, even worse, forever.

164

The future belongs to those who believe in the beauty of their dreams.
Eleanor Roosevelt

What are your dreams? Do you believe you can reach them, or did you give up on them a long time ago? If you want to make your dreams come true, you have to know what you want. Look inside yourself. Who do you want to be? What do you want to have? Where do you want to go?

Dreaming alone is not enough. You have to believe that it's possible to make your dreams come true. Then, my friend, you have to work tirelessly to achieve your dreams. Remember, "If you put a date on a dream, it turns into a goal."

This life is yours. You can do anything you want with it. The sooner you understand this concept, the sooner you can go in the direction of your dreams. Stop sitting around and dreaming of a better life. Take matters into your own hands and start taking action. The results will be remarkable!

165

Be kind whenever possible. It is always possible.
Dalai Lama

Kindness goes a long way in today's word. A good friend of mine once said: "Never miss the opportunity to say kind words." He was right, and I encourage you to live by his words. You will brighten the days of many people. The old saying "What goes around comes around" will play in your favor. The more kindness you spread, the more kindness will come back to you.

If you treat people with patience and respect and are nice to them, you will attract nice people into your life in the long-term. This result alone should be reason enough to be kind to everyone you meet on this journey we call life. Even the rude people you meet deserve your kindness and respect. It's they who need it most. With their rudeness, they are yelling, "I need somebody who loves me too!" Show everyone kindness and respect, even the rude ones. They deserve it.

166

Friends show their love in times of trouble, not in happiness.
Euripides

There is nothing like real friends. Many studies confirm that our social relationships are the number one predictor of our future happiness. Some even show that the strength of our social support network makes us live longer and be less stressed.

Nowadays, we might have 3,478 "friends" on social media but fewer and fewer friends in real life. It's true that when bad things happen, you'll realize who your real friends are. I have lots of friends, but only a handful who didn't turn their backs on me when things didn't go well. Those were my *real* friends.

Troubling times can be great because you find out who your real friends are. It's a liberating feeling. I use times of trouble to filter out my real friends. You should try it.

167

Difficult roads always lead to beautiful destinations.
Benjamin Disraeli

If you've read until here, I think you've got it. For most people, life is not a walk in the park. The best things in life don't come easy. Sometimes, life is damn rough, and we have to accept the truth that we will face problems and setbacks every now and then until our last day on this beautiful planet. But what is also true is that the most challenging roads lead to the most beautiful destinations. The roads less traveled leads us to great treasures. It seems as though we are being tested. Do we really want it? How much do we want it?

If you are on a difficult road right now, keep going. It will be worth it. The destination will be beautiful and even more so because of the person you become on the way. Keep going.

168

Inaction breeds doubt and fear. Action breeds confidence and courage. If you want to conquer fear, do not sit home and think about it. Go out and get busy.
Dale Carnegie

Action is the antidote to a lot of things, but most of all, it's the antidote to fear. Fear of the unknown will never go away. It's a safety mechanism. Our minds want to keep us safe, which is why we fear the unknown. This was great two thousand years ago when it saved us from the countless dangers around us, but it's not so great now. It keeps us from talking to the girl that we like, from writing the email to a potential business partner, from changing jobs. The only way to overcome fear is to face it. Accept it. "Yes, I'm afraid, but I will do it anyway." Go out and get busy. Do the things you fear (except the ones that put you in real danger, of course).

169

There is no man living who isn't capable of doing more than he thinks he can do.

Henry Ford

Most of the time, we unleash our full potential in life-threatening situations or our toughest times. Suddenly, we do things that we never thought we were capable of. We draw energy and strength from unknown places and do impossible things. That alone is proof enough that we are capable of more than we think we are. The challenge is to access this obviously hidden potential when we are *not* threatened. Knowing that we have it is a great start. Now we can get to work and improve bit by bit and day by day so that one day, this potential is at our disposal at any time. Know about it, believe in ourselves, and do it—that's the order.

170

Consult not your fears but your hopes and your dream. Think not about your frustrations, but about your unfulfilled potential. Concern yourself not with what you tried and failed in, but with what it is still possible for you to do.
Pope John XXIII

Pope John XXIII gives us a masterclass about the power of focus. Keep your focus on the positive, and you'll see more of the positive. Concentrate on your hopes and dreams, and you'll be optimistic instead of afraid. Don't think about your frustrations. Know about your potential and abilities. Know that you can do better next time. Don't get stuck in thoughts about past failures. Focus on the future, solutions, and possibilities.

If you focus on success and happiness, you'll see it when it arises. You'll see solutions where other people see problems. You'll see doors where other people see. brick walls. You'll fail, and you'll get better. You'll fail again and again and again, and then you'll succeed.

171

Success is how high you bounce when you hit bottom.
George Patton

Remember how you learn. You fall, and then you get up again. You miss, and then you hit. That is how you grow; that is how you become more resilient, happier, and more successful. You *must* accept that you will fail every now and then. In his book *Geeks and Geezers*, Warren Bennis compared very young and very successful leaders (in their early thirties) to an older generation of leaders (in their seventies to nineties). All of them had at least one thing in common: they all had had at least one significant failure, a real crisis, or a significant loss—their job, their identity, or a person. Both groups saw that moment as a turning point in their lives. They made the best of what happened to them. They saw it as a learning opportunity, a learning experience, or a stepping stone. Success is how high you bounce when you hit rock bottom.

172

Great things are done by a series of small things brought together.
Vincent Van Gogh

Most of us think that we have to do great things or amazing things to achieve our goals and dreams. We overestimate what we can do in a month and underestimate what we can do in a year or five years. We want quick results, fast money, the shortcut. Unfortunately, there is no shortcut on the way to success and great achievements. Every now and then, you might hear of a person that made it overnight, but that's more like winning the lottery. When you look closer, you'll see that the vast majority of great things are the result of consistently bringing small things together. One small win after another accumulates in a big win.

Consistency is the key to success. It's the compound effect that turns lots of small victories into amazing results. Once you can grasp this concept and get away from the addiction to fast results, everything will change.

173

Do your duty and a little more and the future will take care of itself.
Andrew Carnegie

Can it really be that easy? Just do your duty and a little more, and the future will take care of itself? Surprisingly, yes! We've mentioned it before in this book: great things are done through a series of small events. Just do things a little above par, and you will stand out. Go the extra mile, and you will stand out. Most of us are only surviving and not living, so those who do a little bit more than expected are rare. If you do your best every day—even if sometimes your best is only 50 percent—life will automatically take care of itself, and your future will look bright.

Don't strive for perfection. Make the search for excellence your mission. That's enough. In this author's life, a year is comprised of thirty, maximum forty awesome days, 140 days a little above par (doing my duty and a little bit more), 150 totally average days, and twenty real bad days, adding up to a great year. Try it.

174

When you wake up every day, it's like a new birthday; it's a new chance to be great again and make great decisions.
Winnie the Pooh

I hope you agree that in a book where we are learning from the greatest minds, Winnie the Pooh can't be missing. Every day is a new day and a new chance to make better decisions than yesterday. You can reinvent yourself every day. Each day brings with it the opportunity to start a new life. You get to choose your identity at each and every moment. Who do you want to be? What are you going to do? How are you going to improve your life and the lives of the people around you?

It doesn't matter what happened in your past. Yesterday is history. Your future is a clean slate. How are you going to write your story from this day on? If you want to change your life, start a couple of new habits and stick to them. Make some effort and persist, persist, persist. Don't give up. Fasten your seatbelt, and have some fun!

175

Action is a great restorer and builder of confidence. Inaction is not only the result, but the cause, of fear. Perhaps the action you take will be successful; perhaps different actions or adjustments will have to follow. But any action is better than no action at all.

Norman Vincent Peale

One of the secrets to success and happiness is to make things happen. You have to take action. Just talking about what you are going to do is not enough. You can dream big dreams, you can have big visions, and you can draw the most fabulous plans, but if you don't take action, nothing will happen. Just sitting on your sofa, imagining and visualizing a better life is not enough. People who reach their goals are doers who act consistently. Without action, there are no results. Period. If you make a mistake, learn from it and move on. If you are rejected, try again. Become an action-taker.

176

Don't wait for extraordinary opportunities. Seize common occasions and make them great. Weak men wait for opportunities; strong men make them.
Orison Swett Marden

For most of our lives, we wait for one extraordinary opportunity that will make or break everything, and most of us think that life works that way. Well, it doesn't. Winners take everyday occasions—sometimes even occasions that seem impossible—and make them great. Seizing common occasions consistently and making the best out of them will bring you great results. Success is built by consistently doing one small thing at a time. Extraordinary results don't come from exceptional actions. They come from doing everyday actions over and over and over again. Don't wait for opportunities. Look for them. Make them.

177

Continuous effort, not strength or intelligence, is the key to unlocking our potential.

Winston Churchill

We overestimate the power and frequency of huge steps and achievements. We totally underestimate the power of continuous effort while forgetting that most huge accomplishments are many small achievements brought together. We want to save two hundred dollars a month and never get there instead of saving two dollars a day, resulting in saving sixty dollars each month. While we wait for the fantastic event that will change our lives and do nothing, we end up having less than we would have if we had worked on our goals ten minutes a day for one year. Whatever you want to achieve, start now with the smallest step. Tomorrow, take another small step or a small action and then another one. Three hundred and sixty-five small daily actions will almost certainly take you much further than one massive action per week.

178

Every great dream begins with a dreamer. Always remember, you have within you the strength, the patience, and the passion to reach for the stars to change the world.

Harriet Tubman

One of the first quotes every I read was, "If you have a dream, God will give you the power to achieve it." It took me a long time to believe it and a long time to achieve my dream, but today I can say that this quote is true. You can achieve your dreams. Don't let anybody tell you otherwise. It might not be easy; you might encounter setbacks and obstacles, you might have to work hard, and you might have to let some people go. But you already have everything you need. You can do it. I was jobless five years ago. Today, I'm living the life of my dreams. I went after my dreams and didn't let anybody stop me. You can do it too. Start dreaming big and get to work.

179

Spread love everywhere you go. Let no one ever come to you without leaving happier.
Mother Teresa

If you stick to Mother Teresa's rule, you will change the lives of many people, and it really doesn't cost much. As I've mentioned many times before, "What goes around comes around." Spreading love will bring more love back to you, and you should aim to leave everyone who comes in contact with happier. It probably won't work all the time, but it will work most of the time. Sometimes a smile or some kind words will be enough. You want to improve the world? This is a great start. Actually, it's the only way to change the world—with your example and by being kind, person by person. Imagine if everybody did it. What a wonderful world we would live in. Start today.

180

We are all faced with a series of great opportunities brilliantly disguised as impossible situations.
Charles Swindoll

We're coming to the end of the book. What better occasion than this to once more remember that there will be tough times, there will be challenges, and there will be setbacks in our lives. They are part of life. But it's even more important to know that these situations will make us grow and learn. And yes, most great opportunities come disguised as impossible situations or even as tragedies. That is when life puts us to the test. That is when we have to reach inside to draw from our highest potential. That is when champions are born. Never forget it.

Conclusion

That was it, my friend. I hope you loved the quotes, and they helped you a lot! Don't stop here. Now comes the important part: Get to work!

For the longest time, I was only reading inspirational quotes. They made me happy. They gave me hope, but nothing happened.

Inspirational quotes are great. I've read them since I can remember. They helped me when my father died, they helped me when toxic relationships ended, they gave me a boost of happiness when I was in a job I didn't like, they helped a lot when my marriage went sour.

I even read inspirational quotes on Fridays - shortly before going partying and "shooting my lights out" with five to six vodka and Red Bulls. The problem was that after reading the inspirational quotes, I kept on partying as if there was no tomorrow; I kept on being stuck in a job I didn't like; I kept on having toxic relationships and later on, my marriage kept on going sour.

Inspirational quotes are great, but if you don't follow up with action - if you don't make mini changes, if they don't take you out of your comfort zone - you can read inspirational quotes all your life, and you will keep on feeling stuck, miserable and/or unhappy.

Use them to get you into action. Start applying them. "The cave you fear to enter holds the treasure you seek" means absolutely nothing if you don't gather all your courage to enter the cave, to face your fears.

Einstein's definition of insanity, "doing the same thing over and over again expecting different results," is absolutely useless if you keep on doing what you were always doing after reading it, because yes, you saw it coming: You will keep getting the same results.

Einstein's quote was actually the one that got me out of my rut. I finally noticed that if I wanted to change my life, I had to DO things differently. When I stopped just reading inspirational quotes and started doing what they suggested, my whole life changed in a way beyond my wildest imagination.

I went from jobless to bestselling author with more than 300,000 readers. My book, *30 DAYS*, has been translated into over fifteen languages. At the time, I'm writing this the book is rocking Japan, India, Thailand, Spain, Canada and probably China judging by 11,325 reviews on the product page last time I checked.

I'm on TV, radio and podcasts, and best of all is that most of my relationships are super healthy. I haven't had a vodka Red Bull in years, and I am in the best relationship I could imagine.

I still have the occasional setbacks, losses and failures – those are inevitable. They happen. They are part of life. And when they happen…I read an inspirational quote or two.

And then I regroup, make new strategies, look for new alternatives and get back to work.

Try it. It's fun.

I Need Your Help

Thank You Very Much For Downloading My Book!

I really appreciate your feedback, and love hearing what you have to say.
Your input is important for me to make my next book(s) even better.

If you liked the book please be so kind and leave an honest review on Amazon!

It really helps other people to find the book!

Thank you so much!!

Marc

About the Author

Marc Reklau is the author of 10 books including the international Bestseller "30 Days - Change your habits, change your life", which since April 2015 has been sold and downloaded over 250,000 times and has been translated into +15 languages including Spanish, German, Japanese, Russian, Chinese, Thai, Indonesian, Portuguese and Korean.

He wrote the book in 2014 after being fired from his job and literally went from jobless to Bestseller (which is actually the title of his second book).

Marc's mission is to empower people to create the life they want and to give them the resources and tools to make it happen.

His message is simple: Many people want to change things in their lives, but few are willing to do a simple set of exercises constantly over a period of time. You can plan and create success and happiness in your life by installing habits that support you on the way to your goals.

You can connect with him on Instagram, Facebook, or write him an email tomarc@marcreklau.com

Marc's other books

30 Days - Change your habits, change your life

Contains the best strategies to help you to create the life you want. The book is based on science, neuroscience, positive psychology and real-life examples and contains the best exercises to quickly create momentum towards a happier, healthier and wealthier life.

Thirty days can really make a difference if you do things consistently and develop new habits!

More than 250,000 combined sales and downloads since March 2015.

The Productivity Revolution

What if you could dramatically increase your productivity? What if you could stop being overwhelmed and get an extra hour a day to do the things you love? What would finally having time to spend with your family, some alone time to read, or exercise mean to you?

Learn the best strategies to double your productivity and get things done in this book.

Destination Happiness

In this book, bestselling author, Marc Reklau, shows you **scientifically proven exercises and habits** that help you to achieve a successful, meaningful and happy life. Science has proven that Happiness and Optimism can be learned. Learn the best and scientifically proven methods to improve your life now and don't be fooled by the simplicity of some of the exercises!

Love Yourself First!

Having healthy self-esteem is being happy with ourselves and believing that we deserve to enjoy the good things in life, exactly like every other person on this planet. Our self-esteem impacts every area of our life: our self-confidence, our relationships with other, the partner or job we choose, our happiness, our inner peace and even our personal and professional success. This book shows you in a very simple and fun way how to raise your self-esteem by doing some of the little exercises it presents to you.

How to become a people Magnet

"How to become a People Magnet" reveals the secrets and psychology behind successful relationships with other people. Your success and happiness in life - at home and in business -, to a great extent, depend on how you get along with other people. **The most successful people**, quite often, aren't the ones with superior intelligence or the best skills, and the happiest people most times aren't smarter than we are, yet they **are the ones who have the greatest people skills.**

The Life-changing Power of Gratitude

"The Life-Changing Power of Gratitude" reveals the scientifically proven benefits of gratitude. Gratitude is considered **the single best - and most impactful - intervention** of the science of positive psychology. When we are cultivating gratitude, we change the way we feel which changes the way we act, and hence our results.

Being grateful for everything you have in life and even the things you don't have yet **will change everything.**

One last thing...

If you have been inspired by my books and want to help others to reach their goals and improve their lives, here are some action steps you can take immediately to make a positive difference:

Gift my books to friends, family, colleagues and even strangers so that they can also learn that they can reach their goals and live great lives.

Please share your thoughts about this book on Twitter, Facebook and Instagram or write a book review. It helps other people to find 30 DAYS.

If you own a business or if you are a manager - or even if you're not - gift some copies to your team or employees and improve the productivity of your company. Contact me at marc@marcreklau.com. I'll give you a 30% discount on bulk orders.

If you have a Podcast or know somebody that has one ask them to interview me. I'm always happy to spread the message of 30 DAYS and help people improve their lives. You can also ask you local newspaper, radio station, or online media outlets to interview me :)